Frantic Souls

Frantic Souls

Resiliency in life

ROBERT BRUTUS

FRANTIC SOULS
RESILIENCY IN LIFE

Author Credits: Robert Brutus

iUniverse books may be ordered through booksellers or by contacting:

iUniverse
1663 Liberty Drive
Bloomington, IN 47403
www.iuniverse.com
844-349-9409

Because of the dynamic nature of the Internet, any web addresses or links contained in this book may have changed since publication and may no longer be valid. The views expressed in this work are solely those of the author and do not necessarily reflect the views of the publisher, and the publisher hereby disclaims any responsibility for them.

Any people depicted in stock imagery provided by Getty Images are models, and such images are being used for illustrative purposes only.
Certain stock imagery © Getty Images.

ISBN: 978-1-6632-4073-6 (sc)
ISBN: 978-1-6632-4074-3 (e)

Library of Congress Control Number: 2022910348

Print information available on the last page.

iUniverse rev. date: 01/25/2023

Contents

Chapter 1

Foreword

I have known Bob for almost 30 years. We met in Omaha, Nebraska, where we worked for the same payment processing company as software developers. We started as coworkers but quickly became personal friends. It didn't take long to learn from Bob how knowledgeable, entrepreneurial, and creative he is. Sometimes he would tell me about his rental properties and the extensive improvements or fixes he was working on, doing all the work himself. It seemed that there was nothing Bob didn't know how to do. I still remember one of my visits to Bob's home, where he got his guitar and played it for me. I was so impressed at his skill level on that acoustic guitar.

I spent much time with Bob and his family over the years. He would often share stories about growing up in Haiti or about his family members still living there. So, I thought I knew quite a bit about Bob and his life. However, after reading Frantic Souls, I learned that there was so much more to Bob's life than I had ever imagined. This book gave me a deeper understanding and appreciation of Bob's life growing up in Haiti and greater insight into the Haitian people, their history, and the numerous challenges they face. Although we left Nebraska over a decade ago, Bob and I have kept in touch. I consider Bob, a lifelong friend, and it is an honor and privilege to introduce you to Frantic Souls.

Randy Rasmussen

Chapter 2

Preface

Why Frantic Souls

Frenetic is a term used to describe ongoing anxiety, worry, and unease about routine duties. The definition of "Frantic" in the dictionary is "desperate or wild with excitement, passion, horror, and anguish," which accurately sums up how I felt during the events I can remember.

With an easy-to-follow format, "Frantic Souls" conveys compelling scenarios, from commonplace family tragedies to natural disasters and political turmoil.

I've observed that disaster victims typically allow themselves to wallow in regret and suffering. Some people speak up in front of everyone, while others let their emotions paralyze and imprison them. If you are among those who learn from life events and do not let emotions make you weak, you can handle everything life throws at you. You will keep calm and focused.

Over the years, the news media has attempted to capture the complexity of the Haitian people. Sadly, they frequently fall short of accurately presenting its multiple origins, which are rich in theological anomalies and are the foundation of its intricacies.

But slanted media also downplays the immense pleasure of its residents and other parts of its culture as the first independent black nation by emphasizing political upheaval and natural disasters. Its intriguing mythology and expertly prepared cuisine have fed the spirits of those who take the time to recognize its abundance.

Because I'm neither a journalist nor a well-known published author, Frantic Souls purposely lacks the flare of exaggerations to appeal to a specific audience. Such a tactic would decrease the event's authenticity and restrict your ability to empathize with others who are going through similar struggles.

I'll talk about what Haiti represents and how the development and culture of the nation have affected my own experiences several times.

I didn't start keeping note of these happenings to produce a book; instead, I intended to leave a detailed record for my children and future generations to reference. That morphed into an actual book that could be published.

Finding the appropriate framework to describe these interactions grew more challenging over time as the frequency of telling each tale increased.

I'm from a region where most people have a distinct, unfavorable sense of being. From the parade of self-serving governmental policies to mother nature's assault of persistent strikes, I've learned to maneuver through pains with grit and endurance.

The music and songs of the island's inhabitants have ingrained folkloric traditions.

Most of our soulful lyrics are epic tragedies and dismal rhymes, yet despite the underlying melancholy of the chorus, the grounded beat always gives a sense of exhilaration. Whatever your mood, it's a fantastic and joyful beat that may inspire you to dance.

I'm often referred to as the worrier by my oldest daughter. Even though I've been lucky, I frequently picture the worse since I know that anything may happen at any time. But it's not that I constantly worry; it's a sign of awareness and readiness. This style of thinking came about as a result of my discovery that life is a rollercoaster; positive and negative events may and will occur at any time, and I can go about my everyday activities without these events interfering with how much fun they are for me.

Even though many individuals struggle throughout their lives, some seem to have had considerably more painful events that have given them the ability to cope with life's challenges better than others.

Unfortunately, individuals frequently label a group as "cursed" when they witness it suffering more than they should. If such occurs, you should inform these self-appointed judges that you do not feel God has condemned you. This tactic will show them that you know the potential for some of these uncomfortable scenarios.

God will give you the courage to deal with everything life throws at you because He is with you, and you have nothing to fear.

I left the island and came to the United States roughly fifty years ago. My parents gave me my initial name, Jean, and my middle name, Robert.

The English term John, or Jean in French, comes from the Greek name Iohannes, which came from the Hebrew name Yohanan.

I've been called many other things throughout the years, depending on where people are from, such "Zo or Bone" for having been skinny when I was a child to "Jean," "Robert," "Bob," "Bobathan," "Bobby," "Brutus," and "Roberto."

In my culture, many men and women go by the first name Jean, pronounced "Jan," while some women go by the first name Marie. People sometimes pronounce the word "Jean" as "Gene." As a result, I have found myself having to correct them, and I grew accustomed to preferring "Robert."

Of my eight siblings, five are boys, and three are girls; I am the oldest. My younger sister Veronica was born a year after I was. Due to my father's extramarital affair, Melissa was born three months after Veronica. Approximately two years separated the arrivals of Estephan and Natasha. I was around nine years old when Benjamin arrived. I was considered old enough by my parents to serve as his godfather. My parents had to wait nine years before Jayden and Gabriel were born.

I feel this way because I believe God has provided for me. Even though they are my siblings, I have lived a different life and made distinct lifestyle choices. I do, however, consider myself fortunate due to God's favor.

I have generally been a tough person throughout my life. I've learned to be patient with God since He always plans for me. When presented with a challenging circumstance, I reflect on previous ones and how God enabled me to overcome them. He has always given me the courage to carry on.

The likelihood is that you won't be able to predict how your subsequent terrible or difficult circumstance will affect your action plan or what to do when it strikes unexpectedly.

I genuinely hope these tales will motivate you to conquer whatever challenges you may encounter. Reading these stories encourages you to persevere in the face of these difficulties.

You'll have a firsthand understanding of the challenges of maintaining a stern, strong façade while enduring ongoing, silent inner stress through the memories and experiences I've gathered over the years.

I believe God will give you the strength and stamina you need to persevere.

Disclaimer

Several family members have asked me to change people's names so they could maintain their anonymity. My account of the events may differ from what they may have remembered in terms of some details. Of my siblings, I am the oldest.

The financial figures and information presented in this book match the years in which events occurred. Given the current state of the economy and environment, particularly in Haiti, as well as other issues like inflation and political climate change, it would be challenging to replicate these numbers.

Chapter 3

Kindergarten Incident

Survival has never been a straightforward option.

May 25th, 1959, 10:32 AM: I was merely four years old, attending a small private school a couple of blocks away from my childhood home. My father, an auto mechanic, had dropped me off at school that morning using one of the cars he was working on; my mother was at home watching over my younger brother and baby sister.

As kindergartners are prone, I was excited to be lining up to go out for the morning recess. But instead, I watched in horror as a teacher reprimanded a little boy, a disciplinary switch in hand.

The boy had been running too fast and had fallen into the mud. The group of students coming in from recess was a chaotic jumble, the small school principal shouting at them (quite efficiently, even without his usual bullhorn.) Everything seemed perfectly normal as school days went on. And then, as my teacher permitted us to go outside, the children started to break away and run; a game of hiding and seek was already well. I also remember seeing some playing marbles in the dirt yard. Some were jumping ropes while others were kicking a soccer ball to entertain themselves.

Suddenly, a series of rapid popping and banging sounds interrupted us. Teachers began to panic, running outside and physically scooping up as many children as they could bring them back inside, shouting at the rest of us to go back inside right now!! I did not understand the nature of interjecting noise, but I remembered everything, like the moment would never leave me.

I realized that the sounds were gunfire and bullets landing in the schoolyard. Everyone, all the kids, me included – was frightened and crying, mainly because we had never seen the teachers so terrified before. I do not know how, but I remember being back inside the classroom, sitting quietly at my desk, head down, barely breathing. My schoolmates were silent or sobbing quietly, but everyone knew that it was important not to pay attention to us – the teacher had turned off the light and locked the door. We were all waiting for something, but no one knew what.

And then –Bang—Bang—Bang! Someone pounded on the door so loudly it cut neatly through the flurry of honking horns, people screaming outside, and kids sobbing around me. The teacher's harsh voice followed: "stay quiet." It was a whisper, but it filled all of us with dread. It was the fear of every four-year-old: Something scary or the Boogeyman was on the other side of that door, and we were all going to die.

Bang—Bang—Bang! "Open the door," demanded a voice. "Open the door, or I will break it down. Now!"

My heart blossomed with hope because I recognized that voice. I nodded to my teacher and told him: that my father was on the other side. But my teacher insisted I stay in my seat or else. Nevertheless, he hesitantly opened the door.

"Jean, come here," my father said past the teacher. I started to stand.

"All children must remain here in my care until everything is clear," the teacher insisted.

"I will give you one chance," my father growled at the teacher, "to give me my child. Do it now, or you will be sorry." Every four-year-old knew that voice, the 'you're about to get whipped' sound.

But the teacher was insistent. "It is a rule, final," he said firmly. "No one leaves this room until it's clear. So, I suggest you stay here with us, sir."

I knew my father would not accept that, and I bent down to pick up my books. I did not expect my father to punch my teacher in the face and shove him aside. Nor did I expect him to overturn a couple of chairs in his haste to scoop me up and plop me onto his back. We left without looking back to see where the teacher had fallen.

We could still hear gunfire pop and burst around us as my father ran me out of the building to where his best friend – my godfather – was waiting in a 1944 Jeep Willis. (You can imagine almost any older American-army olive-green Jeep, and you will be correct.) My father tossed me into the back seat, leaped into the passenger side, and shouted: "step on it!"

I remember a bullet came close to shattering the windshield and my father's voice trembling as he shouted: "Don't stop! Keep going!" I remember the crowd of pedestrians scrambling to get out of the way. My godfather laid on the horn – and the gas. And I remember the feeling of incredible relief when my father plucked me, curled up and scared silent, out of the back seat and brought me inside my house with my mother, sister, and brother.

It took me years to understand why people were getting shot outside of my kindergarten class and why my father felt it necessary to punch my teacher to get me away. The answer was political.

According to rumors, the day before, the President of Haiti – François Duvalier, a.k.a. "Papa Doc," had suffered a heart attack, most likely due to an insulin overdose. His diabetes had long been a source of heart problems; this one rendered him unconscious for nine hours and probably caused brain damage. His closest associates agreed that he had become paranoid after the heart attack and rapidly devolved into one of Haiti's most brutal and infamous dictators – but that is not important to this story.

What was important is that many people thought that Papa Doc had died from that insulin overdose. They were starting to celebrate – but the Tonton Macoute, Papa Doc's volunteer army, were out to suppress any signs of unrest or disloyalty from the rest of the populace. Gunfire was their weapon of choice, and they used it liberally across Port-au-Prince.

It's worth mentioning what exactly Tonton Macoute means: in Haitian Creole, the name translates as "Uncle Gunnysack – The Sack man – man with the bag/sac" – a character in folklore who roams the streets at night, looking for children who are up too late. If you are out after dark, Uncle Gunnysack would scoop you up into his burlap bag, throw you over his shoulder, and no one would ever see you again.

That is the name the people of Haiti gave Duvalier's army. If it hadn't been for my father coming to rescue me, the Boogeyman, I was afraid, would be on the other side of that door that day in kindergarten.

Chapter 4

Historical Context

François "Papa Doc" Duvalier's rule over Haiti was probably the most impactful in modern Haitian history. He had traveled all over the countryside and campaigned on the idea that the people should share power with their ruler, though he kept a not-very-well-hidden pro-black agenda. He was extremely popular when the people of Haiti elected him, and Duvalier helped eliminate a few acute diseases in Haiti by bringing penicillin to the island.

That plan made instant enemies out of most foreign (white) investors, many mixed-race people (mulattos), the military (supported mainly by Americans, which meant whites), and the church (ditto). Because his enemies were large, well-funded, and everywhere, Duvalier turned to his supporters – ordinary Haitians – and asked the people to volunteer their time acting as his army. That army, the Milice de Volontaires de la Sécurité Nationale or MVSN – "Volunteer National Security Militia" in English – rapidly became one of the most prestigious things an ordinary Haitian man could do with his life.

After that fateful 1959 heart attack and the neurological damage it caused, the MVSN (Milice de Volontaires de la Sécurité Nationale- National Security Volunteer Militia), which he had created just months earlier, suddenly changed. Orders came down from above – orders to beat and kill people suspected of plotting against Duvalier, kidnap the children, gang-rape the wives and daughters of people who seemed to be amassing power, and worse.

Within a month, the MVSN had taken on a new role in Haitian society – as subjugators and peacekeepers – and a new name: the Tonton Macoute. Most everyone who lived in Port-au-Prince knew someone – often a family member, sometimes a friend – either in or was firmly allied with the Tonton Macoute. Their khaki-and-blue uniforms and blatantly carried weapons – sometimes a pistol, but most often a military rifle – were symbols of Duvalier's rule.

But as much their acts were sometimes violent – so – it's crucial that you understand that to everyday people like myself and my family, the Tonton Macoute were still mostly just people trying to help Duvalier keep things running smoothly. Most of the Tonton Macoute were ordinary people who occasionally tended to do horrible things.

Chapter 5

The US Owes Haiti Billions

According to an article written by Bill Quigley, Legal Director for the Center for Constitutional Rights and a long-time Haiti human rights advocate, his views go as follows in this chapter.

Why does the US owe Haiti Billions?

Colin Powell, former US Secretary of State, stated his foreign policy view as the "Pottery Barn rule." That is - "if you break it, you own it."

The US has worked to break Haiti for over 200 years. We owe Haiti. Not charity. We owe Haiti a matter of justice. Reparations. And not the $100 million promised by President Obama either - that is Powerball money. The US owes Haiti Billions - with a big B.

The US has worked for centuries to break Haiti. The US has used Haiti like a plantation. Since its independence, the United States has frequently invaded the nation militarily. It sponsored dictators that oppressed the people, exploited the country as a dumping ground for our economic benefit, damaged their roads and farms, and deposed popularly elected politicians. The US has even used Haiti like the old plantation owner and slipped over there repeatedly for sexual recreation.

Here is the briefest history of some significant United States efforts to break Haiti.

In 1804, when Haiti achieved its freedom from France in the world's first successful slave revolution, the United States refused to recognize the country. The US continued to decline recognition of Haiti for 60 more years. Why? Because the US continued to enslave millions of its citizens and feared recognizing Haiti would encourage a slave revolution in the US.

Following the 1804 revolt, France and the United States imposed a devastating economic blockade on Haiti. Sanctions imposed by the United States persisted until 1863. France eventually used military force to force Haiti to pay restitution for the liberated enslaved people. The compensation totaled 150 million Swiss francs. (For 80 million francs, France surrendered the Louisiana area to the United States!)

The situation has compelled Haiti to borrow money from French and American banks to pay reparations to France. Ultimately, Haiti procured a large loan from the United States to repay the French in 1947. What is the current market worth of the money Haiti was required to pay to French and American banks? More over $20 billion - with a capital B.

President Woodrow Wilson sent troops to invade in 1915. The US occupied and ruled Haiti by force from 1915 to 1934. Revolts by Haitians were put down by the US military - killing over 2000 in one skirmish alone. For the next nineteen years, the US controlled customs in Haiti, collected taxes, and ran many governmental institutions. How many billions were siphoned off by the US during these 19 years?

Between 1957 to 1986, US-backed tyrants "Papa Doc" and "Baby Doc" Duvalier ruled Haiti. The US backed these tyrants financially and militarily because they did what the US wanted and were politically "anti-communist" - now translated as hostile to human rights for their people.

Duvalier stole millions from Haiti and ran up hundreds of millions in debt that Haiti still owes. Ten thousand Haitians lost their lives.

According to estimates, Haiti owes $1.3 billion in external debt, 40% under the US-backed Duvalier.

Haiti imported no rice thirty years ago. Haiti has been importing almost all of its rice. Despite being the Caribbean's sugar-growing hub, Haiti today also imports sugar.

Why? The US and the US-dominated world financial institutions - the International Monetary Fund and the World Bank - forced Haiti to open its markets. Then the US dumped millions of tons of US-subsidized rice and sugar into Haiti - undercutting their farmers and ruining Haitian agriculture. By destroying Haitian agriculture, the US has forced Haiti into becoming the third-largest world market for US rice. Suitable for US farmers but bad for Haiti.

In 2002, the US stopped hundreds of millions of dollars in loans to Haiti. That money was for other public projects like education and roads. These are the same roads that relief teams are having so much trouble navigating now!

In 2004, the US again destroyed democracy in Haiti when they supported the coup against Haiti's elected President, Aristide.

They have used Haiti for sexual recreation, just like the old-time plantations. Check the news carefully, and you will find numerous stories of abuse of minors by missionaries, soldiers, and charity workers. Plus, there are frequent sexual vacations taken to Haiti by people from the US and elsewhere. What is the cost of that? What price would you place on something like this were your sisters and brothers?

US-based corporations have been teaming up with the Haitian elite for years to run sweatshops teeming with tens of thousands of Haitians who earn less than $2 a day.

Like all of us, Haitians made their own mistakes as well. The Haitian people have resisted the economic and military power of the US and others ever since their independence. But US power has forced Haitians to pay great prices - deaths, debt, and abuse.

It is time for the people of the US to join with Haitians and reverse the course of US-Haitian relations.

The current situation provides an opportunity for Americans to confront our country's history of dominance over Haiti and respond in a just manner. This brief history explains why the United States owes Haiti Billions - with a capital B; this is not charity but restitution or justice.

(For more on the history of exploitation of Haiti by the US, see: Paul Farmer, THE USES OF HAITI; Peter Hallward, DAMNING THE FLOOD; and Randall Robinson, AN UNBROKEN AGONY).

Chapter 6

The Beginning

In 1492, before the Europeans came to the island they named Hispaniola, there were many chiefdoms, and Yaguana was one of them. The capital of Jaragua was the last holdout when the Spanish conquered Hispaniola, and the town only surrendered when the Spaniards captured and killed Queen Anacaona in 1503.

In 1697, the Treaty of Ryswick gave the French management of the southern part of the island, now known as Haiti. Today, Yaguana is called Leogane, a hotbed of resistance during the revolution.

In 1931, my mother, Marie Elizabeth Jean, was born a promising young lady.

As her friends and family called her, Eliza left her parents' house at 16. With no formal training, she located a small apartment in Port-au-Prince to live with Simona, one of her best friends.

The two young women made a living by acquiring merchandise from nearby farmers and reselling it at the local market. They noticed many activities coming from one of their neighbor's apartments every Saturday afternoon. Above the door of this apartment were three different colors of lights, and one light bulb at a time would be on various days and at another time of the night.

After seeing the unique decor, Eliza and Simona became very curious. They went to knock at the door and asked the occupant some questions. The first one is why you have all these lights on top of your door. Talking in a manner that confirmed the primary reasons these lights existed.

They provided the young occupant with the perfect opportunity to introduce himself.

"My name is Ornil, he answered with a smirk. There is a perfect reason for the lights."

"No lights indicate that I am not home. The white light states that I am home and not busy. The blue light means I am either available, working inside, or have company; you may knock at the door if you need me. The red light says I am home with a female companion, and I do not want people to disturb me," he explained.

Eliza thought it was very amusing that the young man took that much effort to express his way of life.

During that first conversation, Eliza was conflicted. How often does he entertain female companions to need the construction of such a device? "I need to stay away from him as much as possible," she concluded.

Eliza's concern about his promiscuity was a direct result of her upbringing. Her father was an Episcopal elder and served as a substitute priest in his town when the priest in charge could not make it to the mountain. Her culture taught her to avoid people who do not believe in God and follow Jesus' teachings. Most in her tiny hometown knew Her parents. Her dad would quickly get reports about any deviation in her way of life.

Despite their differences, Eliza and Ornil became friends. She would cook for him and wash his clothes. As time went by, their relationship deepened, and she became pregnant.

Eliza's pregnancy was one of the most humiliating events of her life. As soon as her parents and friends found out, they treated her like she had the plague. They immediately denied her the right to visit her hometown. Those who knew her would call her all kinds of names. Two of her closest friends spat on her at one time.

One day, Ornil visited her parents and promised that he would marry her someday, and he also stated that he would do it in his own time.

Chapter 7

Arrival

On April 1, 1955, Eliza got up very early. She was nine months pregnant and waiting patiently for the magical moment of giving birth to her firstborn.

Eliza got up as soon as the sun shone behind the mountains that day. She put some clothes on, wrapped her head with a handkerchief, and did everything she usually did before embarking on the tedious journey of going to the market. The last thing she grabbed was her basket to put the groceries in and the single dollar she had to ration for the day. The money was enough to cook food for her and Ornil.

On her way to the market, she came across a young hooligan. He told her that someone wanted to see her, adding that this was an emergency. As she wobbled to locate the person who needed her help, the young man shouted jokingly, "Poisson d'avril" (April fool).

It was and continues to be a tradition in many parts of the world and Haiti that people play tricks on others on April Fool's Day. Unfortunately, Eliza forgot what day it was and became very troubled that someone could be so cruel as to play a joke on a pregnant woman who could barely walk.

Later that day, she went into labor at home from the market to her apartment. The apartment was about a two-mile walk from the market, but she got home just in time to have someone summoned for Ornil. He and the neighbors took her to the hospital.

She gave birth to a six-pound, sweet little boy. That's how I came into this world.

Eliza and Ornil struggled to develop the proper name for me. I appeared very skinny, so they gave me the creole nickname "Zo," meaning "Bones."

Even though I was not premature as a baby, my appearance seemed to dictate otherwise.

A few days after coming home from the hospital, I became very sick. My parents spent the following days taking me to see doctors. They took me to every doctor they could find, but none knew what was wrong with me.

My mother had a Christian background, but my dad had a voodoo background. My dad had a plan but knew he must proceed slowly to avoid scaring his young wife. So, he waited.

Every day, my parents would take me to the doctors, who would prescribe different types of medicine.

My mother would throw the prescription away daily because everything she had bought before had not helped. No one seemed to have any idea what was ailing me.

They knew I was getting sicker and thinner every day because I could not eat. My mother breastfed me for an extended period, but that was not enough for me. Sometimes I would eat, and sometimes I would not. The situation became very dire.

One day, my father decided to tell my mother his plan, which meant giving her more details about his religious background.

He told her about how, at one time, the government wanted my grandparents to stop worshiping the loas, as they called their ancestor's spirits. My grandmother's daily actions dictated that the spirits would possess her body. When my grandmother tried to stop, she went mentally unstable. Nobody would come close to her. She lived in the woods by herself and had only one suit of clothes that lasted her years and years. She was continually being possessed by different spirits all the time. Over the years, she got cleaned up. I only met her once. She was a lovely short lady compared to my grandfather, who was at least 6 feet and 2 inches tall.

Chapter 8

Grandpa Normil

In 1960, I was five, and our family lived two blocks from Saint Anne, a Catholic church in Port-au-Prince. I am mentioning this church since it was and remained one of the most iconic places in the city.

Rue cemetery has a straight line to the famous Port-au-Prince cemetery on the east. The locals would give you directions based on how far your destination is from Saint Anne to get around.

The elementary school I attended, "Don Durelan Dumerlin," was on the south side of the church, and the famous High School Lycee Toussaint Louverture, which I also joined later, was on the north side. The People of Haiti named the High School after François-Dominique Toussaint Louverture: a Haitian general named L'Ouverture or Toussaint Bréda; 1743 – April 7, 1803), one of the most protuberant Haitian Revolution leaders.

Louverture demonstrated military and political shrewdness as a revolutionary leader who helped the young slave rebellion change into a revolutionary group. During his life, Louverture first battled against the French, then for them, and then ultimately against France again for the cause of Haitian independence. Louverture is now known as the "Father of Haiti."

One day, a family member came over to drop my grandfather Normil at our house to stay for a few days. What I saw was a tall, aging man. I was trying hard to understand that he was my grandfather since my uncle and dad were extremely short standing next to him.

I later learned the lack of height from my grandmother, who only stood around four feet and three inches tall. His partially wrinkled shirt, neatly tucked in his trousers, projected the impression of a hard-working man who could impress the ladies should he have been younger. The belt that held his pants in place was no more than a very sophisticated knot of a cleanly twisted yellow rope.

His sandals mud crowned by the long road he must have endured catching a ride to our house. As he opened his mouth to speak, I could see where our family resemblance had originated. From the tone of his deep voice and his unique sense of humor, he bent over as he struggled to pick me up and admire me closer. As I looked closer, I remembered the yellow straw hat he wore as I tried to remove it from his clammy head and put it on my own.

He spent some time complimenting my mother for giving him beautiful grandchildren.

"You must be tired from your long trip." Interrupted my mother with a concerned smile, "What can I fix for you to eat" she added. Nothing special, let me rest for a while, and we could talk about the food later, my grandpa retorted.

My mother opened a curtain and showed him the hidden bed. "You may rest here as I send someone to notify Ornil that you are here.

Later that night, my father came home. There was a heated argument between my father and my mother. The disagreement revolved around what to fix for my grandpa to eat and how long he would be around. Our house was small: a big room with a big bed for mom and dad, and the other half had a dining table and chairs. Each night we would move the chairs to one side or stack them on the table to have more rooms to spread out the children's beds. It was understandable the idea of having extra guests created some friction. We had guests before without any issues, but not for an extended period.

My uncle Elijah visited the following day, and the discussion switched to where Grandpa would spend most of his time.

Grandpa needed to be in Port-au-Prince to follow up with doctors regarding his current health conditions. I overheard my father's frustration regarding how he had to help bring my uncle to Port-au-Prince and take care of him. He had helped him go to school while working at an early age. Therefore, if Grandpa needs help, it should have been my uncle's turn to provide housing for him. My uncle geared his points of view toward whether my grandpa's attire was appropriate enough to be a guest at his house. Instead of providing him with new shoes, my uncle thought his sandals would attract criticism from neighbors.

The argument was disappointing as they swapped insults at each other to the point a fistfight was about to break.

My father threatened to pull out a machete to chase his brother out of the house.

My dad finally agreed to have him stay with us. Even today, It continues to be a challenge for me to understand the context from which such an argument would spring from siblings. The event profoundly impacted me, and I am not sure I understood the family relationship and the closeness level between my father, brother, and dad. To this day, I am still looking to attach a proper justification for what happened that day. Living in the US, I have heard horror stories about families who tear each other apart.

That can happen emotionally or physically; now and then, having a blood link does not make the case easier.

People often become better attached to someone who is not blood-related than the other way around. Whether it is a misunderstanding between the two parties or selfishness has found a place to dwell in the heart of one of the parties involved. It is deplorable to witness.

Two weeks after the incident had occurred, my mother had finished preparing breakfast for the family. She left my sister and me alone with Grandpa while she ran to buy a few grocery items. She instructed us to call on the neighbors should something happens to Grandpa.

The older man was not feeling very well. He sat on a bench on the house porch and started to tell my sister Veronica and me some stories. In the middle of the recount, he asked me to fetch him some water. When I returned, I noticed his face looked like someone was experiencing severe pain. I asked him to lie on the bench and lean on my knee. He did for what seemed a very long time. We noticed he was not moving, and I tried to lift his head and realized something was wrong. I carefully asked my sister to bring a pillow so I could rest his head down. I slowly swapped my knee with the pad.

I ran over to one of the neighbors for help. Madam Paul was her name. She came over and did not tell us exactly what was going on. She sent for her husband Paul to fetch my dad. At that point, my mother had returned from her errands at the market.

Several people, including the ambulance, started to show up at the house as the day passed.

My mother then took me aside to explain what had happened. She tried to develop some stories about grandpa having gone to a better place and enjoying no pain. I rudely interrupted her and asked her, "Is grandpa dead?" "Yes, grandpa is dead?" She replied with disbelief.

I kept thinking over the years; whether my uncle and my dad had regretted going so far in their dispute and wished they had spent more time with my grandpa. I am not sure how they have reconciled their differences throughout the years. I know they have not talked to each other regularly.

If it were me, I would contemplate why I would miss the opportunity to spend the last few days with my father before he passed away.

People get involved in meaningless drama over things that are not as important as they appear.

Over the years, my uncle visited the house on birthdays and some rare occasions until he moved to Canada one day.

For a long time, not even his kids knew where he was. Between my uncle and me, things were different. He introduced me to the guitar. I remember him teaching me how to make a tie to dress up for mass. When I was 17, he allowed me to drive a brand-new Jaguar that he was working on for a client so I could impress a girl. He was, instead, a delightful person and very popular with the ladies. He was always proud when listening to his music, playing guitar, and attending clubs.

The Daniel and Joseph incident

It was 1962, two years after the incident with my grandpa; a young man named Daniel came over from Gressier. A small town located about 12.5 miles from Port-au-Prince. He brought some fruits: mango, coconut, and banana. He had with him a young, vibrant boy named Joseph. He was very talkative and eager to learn about life in Port-au-Prince. Before I could utter one word, he asked all kinds of questions. "Do you know I am your cousin? My dad talks about you all the time. "He said. "I heard you are attending a great school, and they have soccer teams and a great church nearby. Can you someday take me to your school with you? I would love to visit. I promise I will be good; please take me there,"; he relentlessly kept asking me. "Is that why you are here," I finally answered. "I'm not too fond of the school I am currently attending." He continued saying with regret. "It is not a formal school. Some old lady comes over every other day and tries to teach other kids about the alphabet and me in the area. I already know all of that.

I do not see myself growing up with a group of farmers. I want to grow up and become a doctor or somebody important." He continued his interrogation without stopping. I had heard about him before, but this was the first time we met face to face. He was a curious fellow. I reassured him farmers are also important in our society. If you want to help your community, I added that you could also become an agronomist and help these farmers. The idea went without any response, and he remained focused on becoming a doctor when he grew up.

After this exciting introduction, I glanced to my left and noticed my mother patiently listening to Daniel and explaining to her the second reason why he came over with Joseph.

Joseph has been running a fever off and on for a long time. Sometimes, he was busy; other times, he had to stay in bed. "The first thing we need to do is have you take Joseph to the doctor, and we can make sure he is healthy enough to attend school," My mother instructed Daniel.

The following Monday, my mother and Daniel took Joseph to the doctors; the boy was diagnosed with a severe malaria case. As much as my mother wanted to help Daniel with his son, there was very little she could do.

Several days passed, and he appeared to have recovered from the illness at one point. We had the chance to play in the yard a little bit, and we even attempted to register him at my school.

As the fever grew and he became weak, they had to take him back to the countryside, where he immediately died of the disease.

That was my second lesson learning about losing someone close to you. I have learned how fragile life can be, and you can be here now, and the next moment you're no longer part of this great play they call life.

Chapter 9

Cautious Father

Since the incident with Daniel and joseph happened, my father became even more overprotective when it came to taking care of us. The following is an excellent example of that.

One day, he heard a very unusual noise. That sound unexpectedly shattered the silence over the heat-burdened night; he believed it came out where my baby brother was sleeping. He wasn't sure whether an animal was in the room or something else had fallen.

"Where in the world is my machete?" He repeated over and over as he aggressively searched all over the house. "Wake-up! Please do your best to keep the baby quiet," Ornil instructed his wife. "Someone or something is walking on the roof," my mother whispered. "NO! my dad answered with frustration. The noise is inside the house, not on the roof."

"Did you look under the bed?" asked his wife.

"Yes, I did! Do you believe I am stupid? Don't answer that," he said with a pronounced frown and confused demeanor. His wife smirked just a little. "This is not funny!" he said, correcting her somewhat cheerful and carefree attitude.

"I know, dear! I am sorry, I cannot help it. I could barely smile because it was only the neighbor's black cat. He does that about this time every night, and I usually go outside while you're asleep to lure it down or chase it away," his wife explained.

"Are you crazy? It is a black cat; you know what they say about black cats!"

(What they say in Haiti is that black cats are like Loup-garou' – a French legend of a human that can change into a werewolf at will. The English meaning of 'Loup' is a wolf, and the word 'Garou' means a man who can transform into an animal. Several cultures have diverse stories about 'Loup-garou.' Haitian folklore includes many anecdotes about witches taking on the form of black cats in the same way a werewolf takes on the form of a lupine.)

"Nevertheless, I will chop it into pieces if it ever comes back – especially if it gets into the house," he affirmed his opinion.

As they continued to argue about a danger, a sudden noise in the kitchen told them that the situation needed a little more attention. My mom and dad ran into the kitchen while the cat jumped to another room to hide underneath their two-month-old sleeping baby bed.

"That's it! That cat will be dead in a few seconds," he said firmly. He grabbed a broom and poked at the cat. The meowing and hissing woke the baby up. The animal's anger level and Mr. Ornil had gotten so high you would think the fight was between a gladiator and a lion in the Roman arena. Maybe it was the added urgency; suddenly, Ornil remembered where he had put the machete.

"Nothing or nobody will threaten my child in my own house. You got balls coming to my house and putting my child in danger. My home is the last house you will ever terrorize." he murmured while crawling to the next room. He maintained his fighting demeanor, and his angry monologue sounded like he was conversing with a well-known person in the neighborhood known as a 'Loup-garou.' The cat finally ran away without getting injured.

The English meaning of 'loup' is a wolf, and the word 'Garou' means a man who can transform into an animal. Several cultures have diverse stories about 'loup-garou.' (They say in Haiti that black cats are like Loup-garou – a French legend of a human that can change into a wolf at will. Haitian folklore includes many anecdotes about witches taking on the form of black cats in the same way a werewolf takes on the form of a lupine.) "Nevertheless, I will chop it into pieces if it ever comes back – especially if it gets into the house," he affirmed his opinion.

Even though it seemed unimportant or straightforward that night, he did not leave anything to the imagination to avoid his potential fury; he might unleash it if necessary.

Numerous enigmatic superstitions have existed and still do in Haiti. Whether or not your degree of education gave you access to scientific answers, plenty of dishonest behavior made you doubt everything around you.

Both the cat and the infant were unharmed when the cat left. The incident was entertaining while also putting all of us on edge.

We sat down and listened to a few stories as the stress and passing of time subsided. In some of these circumstances, things did not go as pleasantly as they did for us.

Chapter 10

Loss of a Friend

My father worked as an auto mechanic and owned a repair shop. His old friend Andre Dante had a son, Carlos Dante.

Carlos came to the shop six years prior. Being a good friend of the family, Carlos' mother recommended him to my father. The store usually had twelve to fifteen men working, depending on the season and the number of trucks needing repair.

Andre and Martha Dante, Carlos' parents, and my father agreed to let Carlos work for my dad and learn the trade. Young men outside of Port-au-Prince did not have a lot of choices when it came to the type of work: some could work on a farm, go to school to learn a trade, or learn a career working with someone their family knew. That was it.

Unfortunately, young women had very few choices: Desperate parents turned their kids to families who were better off financially. The most popular trades worked in an automotive shop as a mechanic, on a construction site as a house builder crew member, Taxi, or truck driver. The children would work as housekeepers and maids in exchange for room and board. This arrangement allowed them to live in better conditions than their own families.

Carlos' parents, Andre and Martha, were long-time friends of my father and mother, even before I was born. There was some friction between our two families because of who Andre was. Andre was one of the most feared voodoo priests in the area, and people feared him because of what he could do to affect people's lives or make them miserable.

For instance, Andre was the equivalent of the top mob boss in Chicago. He was dominant, people said, and Andre could send his minions to torture people if they did not submit to his demands. The worst part was that, though everyone talked about it and the stories spread from person to person, no one could prove he was behind what he did. Andre's victims were everywhere.

Andre Dante was like a sword. But, on the flat side, many people have confidence in him. Some consult with him to get herbal medicine and advice. Others came to him when they wanted to hurt someone.

I am unsure if my father agreed to hire Carlos because of fear or because he and Dante were friends, but I know the negotiation took a long time before Carlos became a permanent employee.

I became close to Carlos; he was like an older brother. He taught me a lot about girls, and we frequently went to the movies together. He was the one who helped me sneak out with a truck, so I could learn how to drive. Carlos also taught me how to weld a broken chassis. He taught me how to use gas flame and electric arc for different welding materials.

One sweltering summer day, I was part of the shop crew because I was on vacation from school. It was the summer of 1969, and I was only fourteen years old. Carlos was particularly good at what he did and had risen to third in the rank of welders in the shop. My father was considered the best welder, and a gentleman named Tony Valentino was also second-best. During those days, many truck owners. Some branches of the government brought their transportation and road construction trucks to the Ornil Phillip Shop. After a long trip from Leogane or Jacmel to Port-au-Prince, it was inevitable that we would receive trucks with broken chassis that needed repair because of the roads' conditions.

Before coming to the shop, the truck owner would remove the truck's transportation box or trailer. Five to eight of us would then grab the appropriate wrenches, crawl under the chassis, and start to remove big bolts. Then, as soon as the vehicle entered the store, my father would negotiate the repair price.

Sometimes it took three or four of us to unscrew one big bolt. If it were too rusty, we would insert the wrench inside a giant metal tube and pull it simultaneously until the screw came loose. It was hard work. Once we remove the broken part, we would take it inside and heat it in a handmade charcoal furnace. One could increase the heater by cranking or turning a handle that ran an internal fan underneath the fire. Someone had to stand there and crank that handle the whole time the chassis was inside the furnace. Once the frame was hot enough, one or two people would hold it while a third person used a sledgehammer to straighten the metal out. We would repeat this process until we obtained the desired shape.

We did not have proper cutting tools to cut the chassis, so we adopted an extraordinarily tedious and dangerous process. One person would hold a significant chisel in one hand. In contrast, another person lifted a sledgehammer as high as possible and dropped it on the blade, hopefully onto the center of the tool, with all the force and energy he could muster. If you miss the device, it means an uncomfortable trip to the hospital. It usually took two to three hours, sometimes more, to cut one foot of chassis. Then, after the enclosure had been removed from the vehicle, reduced, heated, and straightened, it was time to weld it back onto the truck.

That day we were arc welding using electrodes made of carbon that resulted in too high temperatures capable of melting any metal. Instead, the metal formed a pool of molten material that, when cooled, became an active joint that fixed the chassis back onto the truck. The electrical spark that the electrodes produced was so intense it could damage your eyes if you stared directly at it.

The truck we were working on was an eighteen-wheeler. The tires were so big I could hide behind one without fear that someone would see me on the other side. Carlos stood between the tires to do his magic, and I turned away to avoid looking at the spark.

As soon as Carlos dropped the protective mask, I could hear the electrodes buzzing. I could usually tell if the wire got stuck, making a more lasting buzz. But I heard the faint sound of someone's hand hitting the tire next to me.

Carlos tried desperately to reach my shoulder. He was going through deadly electrocution without my knowledge as he was in extreme distress. As soon as I realized what was happening, I began screaming as loudly as possible, "Turn the power off! Turn the power off! Turn the power off!" My father ran inside and turned the power off while several other people rushed over and pulled Carlos's limp body underneath the truck.

The bottom of Carlos's feet turned white as a piece of paper. All we could do at first was stand beside him and watch him as he began to die. Finally, we placed him in a car and rushed him to the hospital, thinking we still had time. But unfortunately, it was too late. We did not have a phone to call an ambulance, and we did not have any CPR or Cardiopulmonary Resuscitation knowledge.

Carlos was dead. How were we going to break the news to his father, Andre? The fear and anguish I felt over Carlos's death became more petite than the fear of what his dad would do to my father.

Following this, my father went through a period of terror that I will never forget. We visited several other voodoo priests to discover something that would counteract whatever Andre might throw at us, but no one seemed to have any answers.

Fortunately, several years passed, and nothing terrible happened to my father or family, at least nothing we could attribute to Andre.

During this period, I had the opportunity to view the world of voodoo up close, giving me a unique perspective and learning more about this religion.

The term voodoo is not a term people use in Haiti. Some people refer to it as "white magic"; People prefer to use "black magic" when wishing harm upon someone.

The secret act or the intimate knowledge of voodoo can involve planting items in a field or concocting a potion made from herbs, spices, and various plants or organic substances. When someone injects poisonous medicine into another person's skin, it can produce sickness or even simulated death. For example, the native used toxic portions of the pufferfish.

There is a certain level of secret and mysterious knowledge involved in voodoo. Practitioners can find natural remedies for illness in plants scattered around the island. Their names and what they can do to a person are knowledge passed from one priest to the next during initiation and training. The results can seem magical. However, they are replicable by anyone with the right expertise. It does not matter whether one is a voodoo believer or not.

Chapter 11

Bully on the Loose

Several years later – 1971 – François Duvalier gave way to his son, Jean Claude Duvalier, a.k.a. "Baby Doc." That was also the year I, as it seemed everyone eventually did, came face-to-face with a Tonton Macoute in the wrong way.

I was driving a 1944 Jeep Willis as my dad picked me up during the kindergarten incident. It was a bright Saturday afternoon in the middle of summer; my father, brother, and I left my dad's shop to go home. As customary, we usually stop at one of the bakeries to take something special for the family– often a meat-stuffed croissant we called "pate" and some very delicious bread. I dropped off my dad and brother in front of the bakery and went to find a nearby parking spot.

When I returned to the bakery, I noticed my father was distraught with a young man with whom he had what appeared to be a very heated argument.

"This girl has been waiting for hours; she didn't do anything to deserve that!" said my dad.

"It is none of your business! Do you know who I am? I can do whatever I want!" retorted the man. "You keep interfering; you probably get the same treatment."

As they continued to argue, some customers began to boo the young man, and he finally left, looking ferocious and bitter. "What happened?" I asked my father.

"You should have been there; this guy came out of nowhere, grabbed this little girl, pushed her out of line, and attempted to take her place. When she objected, he slapped her so hard that the poor girl fell on her back and started to cry.

Everyone who saw the incident instantly hated him, and I told him off, and the crowd booed him out!" my dad explained.

After purchasing our merchandise, we all climbed up to the jeep. As I continued to drive, we realized someone was following us. The car behind us was pulling close. I could hear the loud honking, and the driver waved a gun out his window. Then, we heard a voice screaming, "This is the last time you will ever embarrass an authority figure; I swear to God, I will kill you. Pull the car over! You coward, pull the car over, you coward!" shouted.

Other drivers began honking, unhappy with the situation (and mostly unaware of the danger), and a crowd began to gather, running behind, expecting to see something go down. I slowed down, but my father had other plans. I was terrified when I saw the gun – pointed straight at my father. And, as the guy at the wheel, probably me.

"Do NOT stop this car!" he snapped. "Turn left." "Where are we--" I started, and he cut me off.

"To the palace." I drove, probably quite carelessly, but I do not remember precisely, and did my best to ignore the gun that kept appearing in my mirrors. The palace was opposite my house, and while it was not that far, it was not a quick place to drive through. The crowd running along behind us was getting more substantial – and louder! We could not tell if they were cheering Tonton Macoute or booing him.

Two armed guards stopped me as I stopped at the palace gate a few minutes later. "Who are you here to see?" My dad was ready for the answer: "Major Andre." "Proceed."

I watched as the massive metal gate swung open, and I thought we were safe – but then I watched as the maniac following us was waved right on through, still on our bumper when I stopped. I was confident we would get shot right here in the courtyard, like criminals in execution – but as God's grace had it, Major Andre happened to be walking across the yard, preparing to leave, when my father yelled for him.

The volunteer soldier and my father approached Major Andre simultaneously and began to speak rapidly. "CALM DOWN," said the Major sharply. Once silence descended, he took my father – a long-time friend, thank Heaven – off to one side and talked to him for several minutes. Then he took the soldier aside and spoke to him for several minutes. Then he brought them back together.

"Do you know who this is?" the Major asked the soldier, who shook his head quietly. "Without this man," the Major gestured at my father, "We're all screwed. He is the mechanic that keeps all our most important vehicles working. Why would you want to kill him? He does not carry a gun like you and me, but he is one of us. I suggest you leave him alone –; if anything happens to him or any member of his family, I will hold you personally responsible."

The soldier gave my family one of the most malice-filled 'smiles' I have ever witnessed and holstered his gun in a way that suggested it was the last thing he wanted to do. Then, as he climbed back in his car and left, everything he did scream, I want you DEAD.

I never saw that man again. Thank God.

I later asked my father if he was a Tonton Macoute, and he told me he would never be. Of course, he fixed their trucks, just like he set anyone else who paid him. That is how he kept his family safe, but that was the entire extent of their relationship – personal (and valuable) friendship with Major Andre.

My parents were renters until I was 11, when they built a house, as most people were. We moved to different locations very often. During that period, the political situation was not stable as usual.

We had constant and unscheduled power outages; it was a scary moment when the lights went out. First, the lights would dim and flicker constantly before everything went completely black. Occasionally, we could hear gunshots outside. It was a frightening moment for most kids.

I remember sometimes the radio would broadcast songs about fire. No one could explain the situation to me, and why would anyone sing a song about the house being on fire? These conditions have left a mark on my frantic soul.

My father was a hard-working man who would do anything to ensure he acted to protect his family. He worked with what he had and did not deprive us of anything.

Every morning, he left the house between six and seven and did not return until the sun was down, usually after six or seven PM. If he comes to the house during the day, something must have gone wrong.

I remember one of these unfortunate occasions when he came home with a sad face one day.

I quickly noticed his left hand was all wrapped up with hospital gauze. My mother rushed toward him, carefully asked what had happened, and wished to inspect the injured hand.

He painfully tried to explain what had occurred, only to get interrupted by the sharp pain vibrating through his whole arm.

After the healing had taken place, we realized the car door had crushed three of his fingers. He swallowed his spit and said: "One of his clients closed the door on his hand quicker than he had time to remove it out of the way." His hand has never been the same since then.

Chapter 12

Formative Years

Our family moved regularly when my parents added my last two youngest brothers during my formative years. When we moved from the north to the south side of town, an industrial area, I met a different type of worship for the first time.

Our new landlords were Baptists, and they took us to a Baptist Church every Sunday morning and later put us in Sunday School. That was the first time I came face to face in contact with worshiping Christ, the Savior.

Our home was simple. It contained merely one room and a porch, which was standard. The house was not too far from the railroad; it was probably around 500 to 1000 feet from the railroad tracks.

The cargo trains came from Leogane and other parts of the country and carried sugar cane. They process the sugarcane into sugar and alcohol. When the trains went by, the children would run alongside and pull the sugar canes out of the train. The train would hurt some people; they lost their legs, arms, and sometimes their lives. The other sad thing about this place was that we got tons of water into our home every time it rained.

When the flood came, my parents put a mattress on the table and put us children on top. The water would go halfway up the house, and if they did not have time to pull up the mattresses, they took care of us first. If the beds did become soaked, we did not have money to replace them, so we had to let them dry in the sun the next day and sleep on them, although they smelled awful.

The most important thing that happened during this period of my life was that I met the Lord. We were still Catholics, and they allowed my aunt and me to be Godparents to my mother's next son because they trusted me. We took him to the church when Paul was born, and I represented him.

We relocated to a place across from my father's workshop. Our lives started to improve as the shop began to bring in more money. More young men have found work, and his reputation as a dependable shop to maintain trucks and vehicles has already started to spread.

My father wanted to build a house and move to the mountainous area of Port-au-Prince. Since my little brother was so small, I used to play tricks on him and say, "Hey, if you don't give me your meat, I'm not going to pull you up the mountain."

We had to climb the mountain where my father was building the house. It was so high that we had to pull the rope to get him there, so I told him I would not give him the line so that he would give me all his meat.

My brother Paul was still tiny; we had an experience that we believed was caused by a Loup-garou.

When we woke up, my brother was in a different house room than he had been the night before. No one knew how he had gotten into the other room, but there was a black cat under his bed, and when my father tried to get it out of the house, the cat attacked him and fought him. My father finally got the cat out of the house, and my brother was unhurt, but it was a very frightening experience because we believed the spirits had invaded our home in the form of the black cat.

The first year we moved there, I passed my exam to have ~my first Communion. My school building even had a history of voodoo behind it. People believed that the man who founded the school was married to a mermaid and that nobody could see him on Tuesdays or Thursdays. He had a lot of money, and nobody knew where he worked or how he got his money, but he built schools in the country and gave them away to the government at no cost.

During my school years in Haiti, I remember the first year I passed and the second year failed. In the third year, I had a tricky teacher with us. It was so hard that we had to know our lesson. He would take us underneath the almond tree in the schoolyard. All the kids would take almond tree leaves, make them into tiny cones, put them in our ears, sing songs that we didn't know our lessons, call us asses' ears, and tell us that we have significant ears.

Our school system had multiple divisions: infantry one and two, preparatory one and two, elementary one and two, and two "pre-high schools," one and two. In elementary one, my teacher gave me a lot of courage; he had a lot of confidence in me, and he always told me how good I was, so he had a lot of impact on my life. I had another teacher who was so tiny, and the next teacher I had who impacted my life was a teacher in my middle school years.

When we moved to our house, my father built a room for the spirits, a unique home in the room's back corner. It was not too big, but he had a specific home for them, a place for the spirits.

Before my dad could own his automotive repair shop, I remember him working as a regular mechanic for other shop owners. One of these shops was located one block from a popular police station and the only roundabout or circular intersection in town. The entrance had a wide gate. The yard was dirt-covered, and the mechanics lined up several rows of trucks while they performed different repairs. A wall made of cement blocks separated some of the noises from the primary street of Boulevard Jean Jacques Dessalines.

During break time, several workers lined up their chairs against the wall as they joked around and ate their mid-day meal. In the middle of that memorable day, a space became available, and one of the mechanics went outside to back up a truck that was ill-parked in traffic. The vehicle was massive and loaded with different types of cargo. The driver could not see the person given direction, nor could he hear him screaming the word "STOP" multiple times.

By the time he finally stopped, it was too late, and the truck with the cargo hit the wall and ran over the person given direction and three other workers sitting there. The car had crushed their bodies beyond recognition.

The event was sad and miraculous for him simultaneously because he was sitting at the exact location. He was not part of the accident because he and other co-workers decided to get up seconds before it happened.

Until today, I still can see my dad walking toward our door with his shoulders swinging from left to right like a pendulum clock to bring us hard-to-consume news. He had a distinctive walk, and my mother always bragged and made a joke about it.

These experiences have kept me on my toes. I never knew, nor would anyone know, what would happen next. I learned to be resilient and rely on God to help me handle whatever comes next.

Chapter 13

Voodoo Environment

For a good reason, Voodoo has always been Haitian culture's essence and center. It is still being practiced openly and behind doors. When the sounds of drums, the humming of folkloric songs, and exotic dances joined together to create a delight for the native atmosphere, those who practice voodoo will never forget January 1, 1804, their Independence Day, in their unique way. It has helped them become the first black republic in the world proudly.

Nationally, most Haitians prepare a special dish for Independence Day. Besides sharing the worldwide celebration known as New Year's Day, they have something even more precious that keeps them awake on New Year's Eve. As confetti, balloons, smashing of glasses, laughter and resolutions mingle in the ballrooms, a distinctive smell of squash soup marinated with spices, onions, and meats, always finds its way to every Haitian nostril home. They have faithfully kept the soup tradition for centuries, and most Haitians feel the same about voodoo.

The word voodoo itself is an African name for spirits. The Frenchman Savant Moreau de Saint Mary made the term famous just before the French Revolution in 1791, and it probably did have a different meaning for the French people.

For the Caribbean Indians, it could be the worship of the snake. But for Haitians, the channel led them to freedom—a world of spirits they trusted to protect them. In the past, different government systems have tried to deprive them of their religious practice, but it could only engrave the memories deeper and deeper in their hearts.

They knew that their ancestors came from different tribes of Africa, including the Nago, Fans, Ibos, and others. It is something that they hold dear to their hearts.

Chapter 14

My Grandmother

My father once tried to explain his mother's history of mental illness to me.

I recall him telling me that one day, folks in the house where he grew up began to hear horse paws and hoofbeats. Desmil, my father's uncle, flung open the front door to see what was outside. On a black horse, he noticed a tall, broad-shouldered guy rushing toward the front gate. Desmil didn't know the horseman, but when he burst his horse into a canter with a fast judder of the reins, he recognized it was his nephew Oramil. When the horse came to a halt, Oramil Phillip got off the saddle and hugged Desmil before instructing the youngster to tether the animal to the nearest post.

Oramil was dressed casually in a long-sleeved red shirt and blue pants. He wore a crimson scarf with white stripes around his neck. While waiting for Desmil, he removed his palm-made hat and tucked it under his arm. "Come on in," a voice behind him said. "Normil, is that you?" Oramil said with a grin on his face.

"You haven't altered a bit, my goodness," he exclaimed as he approached his uncle. "You haven't either," Normil teased, holding the door wide for him. "Aren't we finally going to do it this year?" "questioned Oramil, taking the chair Normil offered him.

"I've been sending invites to all family members since last year." Clara, Aunt, will be the mambo this year, and I suppose you and I will be the Hougan (ceremony masters)," Normil's wife, Zabelie, remarked. "I think I'm ready for that," Oramil said. "I brought ashes and chalks for the invocational design." "I even purchased a new bell and two goats for the sacrifice," he explained. "Please let me know where they are, and I will pick them up later in the day," Normil stated. "You are such a responsible man, Oramil, my nephew."

"You'll locate them 500 feet distant from the Loas house.

"The loas (ancestor's spirits) dwelling was a huge mapou tree on the north side of the village cemetery. Its branches stretched 150 feet from south to north and around 75 feet from east to west.

The shrubs were so dense that people in the nearby region suspected that people from another world had spent years living there. Around three o'clock that afternoon, it was usually dark under the tree, and no one ventured to approach it.

Chapter 15

My Grandparents – Father's Side

On the morning of my first trip to Trouin near Jacmel, the roosters, locusts, and dogs from across the hill sang the last note of their usual morning symphony. The sun's rays illuminated my bed to end one of the most memorable nights. I slowly and unconsciously gave my body a long and rejuvenating stretch While rubbing my eyes to clear my vision.

I turned over three times to find my head buried underneath my blue and white cotton soft pillow. As my soul tried to depart my aching body, two cold fingers pinched my lonely little toe to shock me from my delightful morning slumber. I tossed my pillow across the room to discover my dad woke me up as he shuffled out of the shower. "Time to get out of bed," he snarled. "Remember, today is the big day. We are going to Jacmel. "I know," I answered. "How can I forget? We had a party last night. I just got to bed a few hours ago."

It was the summer of 1960, and I was five years old. I was the firstborn of a family that had already grown to six members. The time had come for my dad to take me on an essential journey. That morning, a group of more than seventeen people had crowded into our one-bedroom apartment. They danced, clapped, screamed, rejoiced, and displayed every chapter in the book of human feelings and emotions.

The best words that describe my being that morning were excitement and confusion. I was confused because I did not have the slightest idea of what had happened the night before. I was excited to take the trip because I looked forward to seeing my grandmother for the first time.

I forced myself out of bed and grabbed a towel and my little red brush to prepare for the trip. My mother wandered around the house, ensuring we had everything we needed for our journey. "Can I go too?" whispered my little sister, Veronica, as she followed my dad. "You are not going," he bellowed. Th he playfully picked her up and tossed her in the air. "You will stay with uncle Desmil while Bones and I get lost in the forest. No!" he said. "I will go wherever you go," answered Veronica in a harsh and desperate tone.

November 1, 1945: My family lived in Trouin, Haiti's Ouest region, about 24 miles southwest of Port-au-Prince, the capital. It was still dark outside when the occupants of a small house on top of a hill began their day. Normil Phillip, his wife Zabelie, and their kids, Lozanne and Elsainis, awakened early to start a critical day.

It was the day that the family was to have the annual voodoo ceremony on their property. My grandmother Zabelie went to a small acajou cabinet to count her wares, including dried herring and little bundles of tobacco leaves. Finally, she found a piece of tobacco she liked, crunched it into her short bamboo pipe, and lit it as she made her way to the table, looking for the coffee pot.

Meanwhile, Normil went to the next room to count the clairin bottles, colorless alcohol like moonshine corn whiskey. Finally, he found a small glass and poured himself a drink while ensuring they had enough people to show up that day.

My great uncle, Desmil, and my aunt Lozanne got dressed and unlocked the front door. They could hear the roosters crowing. The pigs were already making their familiar oink sound to ensure that no one had forgotten them. It was so early that the sun was only a tiny reflection of its rays behind the mountains. Desmil went down the hill through the banana field to feed the hungry pigs, while Lozanne ran to the left of the taches-covered house, searching for the family's white horse. He brought the horse over and attached its rope to a pole in front of the house. Lozanne ran back inside to announce that he had done his duty.

"I could have sworn that I bought fifty gallons of clairin last month," said Normil in a harsh tone. "How come we only had forty-nine?" You probably drank it," answered Zabelie while she puffed up a few clouds of smoke in the air. "There is no way I could have drunk that much clairin...unless...Lozanne!" He screamed. "Did you touch any of that stuff?" His son answered, "Desmil and I did try a couple of drinks, but I doubt we consumed that much." "I guess our kids are getting too old," said Normil jokingly.

"The time has come," said Normil in a loud voice. "I will go and get the goat for the sacrifice." An older woman stumbled back a step as the man, and his horse galloped away, creating a blinding cloud of dust that forced everyone to return to the house.

The older woman's name was Lozanne. She was my father's sister and had been the mambo of the ceremony at midnight. As soon as she got inside, she gathered everyone to explain that something terrible would happen that day. You see, old Lozanne never lies. She became known as a clairvoyant woman. Everybody sat and listened to her—everyone but Zabelie, who refused to believe anything would happen. She was more concerned about the message received during last year's ceremony, contemplating the unavoidable side effects of a chain of senseless death.

"I will destroy all of you. - I will destroy add of you if you do not feed my legion next year." These words kept screaming in her mind. But before Zabelie could open her mouth to say anything, the message was clear. Silence filled the room, and everyone started to panic. Lozanne crossed her leg and puffed away on her pipe, finally breaking the silence to say, "I wish there were something I could do to prevent it. We're doomed."

As they comforted each other, they heard a piercing scream outside, then the sound of a horse, followed by someone falling and a cry. No one knew what was happening yet. They rushed out, and the sight of smoke made them forget why they had come out.

Normil had been on his way back. He was close to the house. But for some reason, the last 500 feet seemed to take forever. He was gasping for air. The horse he was riding had collapsed two miles back, and some shot him in the legs. The poor man had no choice but to run away, leaving his horse behind. He wanted to get home as soon as possible to tell the family about the government's voodoo decision.

He stopped to wipe his face off the blinding sweat that blurred his vision. He looked up, saw the smoke, and understood that the family probably or should know about all the incidents by now. He wrapped his beautiful white shirt around his waist, took a deep breath, and rushed to the front gate.

"We must stop everything," he shouted as he collapsed. Zabelie poured some water on his head to wake him up. "Everybody gets inside," he said wearily.

The government had ordered the local sheriff to investigate any suspected voodoo activity. The sheriff and his violent men were on their way to Phillip's home, and it was too late for them to hide anything. They had just burnt two houses down the road and shot two peasants and some animals, including Normil's gorgeous white horse.

Zabelie ordered the master of the ceremony to go ahead with their plan. "Are you crazy?" Lozanne whispered to Zabelie. "We can't do that! They will destroy us and our home."

"We will see about that," replied Zabelie as she grabbed Normil's machete from him and ran to the mapou tree. She circled the tree seven times and suddenly knelt at its bottom. As she hit the machete against the tree, she lifted her head and screamed at the top of her lungs.

A snake came down from the tree and looked directly at her. She felt a magnetic power that compelled her to dance until she fell unconscious on the ground. Two men came over and carried her to the next-door neighbor's house. They could not take her back to her own home because the sheriff and his violent men had burnt everything.

From that day on, Zabelie Phillip never spoke another meaningful word. Her family held onto their hope for a long time, not knowing that she would remain mentally insane for the rest of her life. They secretly tried to invoke the spirits they had been worshiping for years, asking them to cure her.

She would wake up every morning, go straight to the mapou tree, and stare at the snake for hours and hours. At night, when a full white moon rose in the sky, she would lay on the ground and whistle for hours. A purring growl seemed to come from the tree, creating a harmonious sound.

It was a regular ritual to become her life for the next fifteen years. One day, she went away, and no one knew how she was living because she never returned to the house again.

Years before, in 1921, the Phillip family had a voodoo ceremony. During the festivities, Zabelie became possessed by a spirit named Damballa, and she went to the top of the mapou tree, dancing and singing.

From then on, the tree became the permanent house of the loas. Rumors spread regarding an enormous snake that once lived there, but no one had seen the snake.

Phillip's family believed the snake was natural since the spirit identified himself during the 1921 ceremony. They used goats for sacrifice because uncle Oramil had received instruction in his dream.

The Phillips had many animals, but they had to have a specific kind of goat for the sacrifice. In fact, for a long time, they owned twelve hundred acres of land. They used some of it for farming, mostly corn millet, coffee, tobacco, sugar cane, mango, and coconuts. They used the rest of their land for cattle animal horses for their animals.

Tilling the field was the primary source of social contact for most men. So, they organized a "coumbite," during which all men willing to help their neighbors cultivate their field would come over when they heard the lambi (conch shell).

The women were primarily responsible for drawing water and carrying it from great distances, beating the laundry in the riverbed, and doing all the marketing. That was the custom passed to them from generation to generation. The idea came in cacos and corvées since it was unsafe for the men to go to the market.

The word "corvée" originated in Rome, reaching the English language through France. It refers to unpaid labor that lasts for limited periods, typically only a certain number of days each year. It is common for people to use the word as a work barter system in Haiti. A group of men gets together to help till each other's farmland. The women learned to live with it since they enjoyed bargaining and gossiping to give it up.

Chapter 16

Looking for a Cure

My father believed I was sick because Lozanne did not want him to marry my mother. Therefore, he had to go home to find out who had caused his son's mysterious illness. Since my mother did not have any cure anywhere else, she accepted the idea. She stayed home while my father took long trips to the mountains, traveling on foot for days to see the voodoo priests.

When my dad arrived at the voodoo priest's house, the priest, Hougan, invited him to sit in a small chair. He instructed my dad not to say anything. Instead, Hougan told him why he came to visit him.

"Did you bring a candle?" the hougan asked my father. My father said yes, as my father proceeded to light them. The hougan put a cross on the table and added a white dish and a white tablecloth. Nobody else was in the house, just the voodoo priest and my father.

I saw pictures of various saints in the corner of the room, such as St. Jacques and others. The painting on the wall showed a man on a horse dressed in armor. The horse was pictured reared up, with his front feet off the ground. The rider almost looks like he is falling off the horse, but he is not. Fire is under the horse, and a long sword is in the rider's right hand.

There was also a picture of two distinctive spirits—a black Virgin Mary and a white Virgin Mary.

The Hougan started shuffling the cards before laying them on the table. It was a regular deck of cards, but he had his way of reading them. Each card had a special meaning. If seven spades appear, it means that someone will die. If hearts show up, it means that people are in love. The diamonds represented money, and clubs indicated someone was sick.

The Hougan picked the cards up and laid them down one after another. As he told my dad his life story, Oramil realized this person was wasting his time. He got up and gathered his belongings, and left.

The next priest, my father, visited and said to him, "Well, I see you've got a sick kid." My father said, "That's right; what do you want to do about it?" The voodoo priest replied that he guessed my father wanted to know who did it. He told my father it was because of my dad's mother that I was sick. All the spirits wanted to get into our house.

Some would say that my dad's sister doesn't like his wife, and so forth. Still, my father sought out other voodoo priests. The strange thing was that these people would tell him a different story.

One day, my dad encountered a Hougan with a very enthusiastic personality. His name was Andre Dante. Andre informed him that the best thing to do was worship the spirits in his house. Hougan told him to build a shrine or a sanctuary in his home and pray to the nerves.

He had walked hundreds of miles and seen all the priests he could see, and they all told him the same thing. They explicitly said that his son would not improve until his sanctuary was complete. So, he put items together to build the correct shrine according to his instructions.

So, my dad went downtown and bought a box. He had two boxes; one was probably about three feet tall, and the other was four feet tall. One of the boxes had doors, and the other one did not. The one with doors had a glass to see what was inside. He also had candles in different colors; black, red, and white.

When he got all the voodoo images, he could find them. He put them in the corner of his house. Every morning he lit a candle, threw water on the floor, and sprinkled water on the front of the house. The priests told him this would keep the evil spirits out of the house.

He did everything the voodoo priests had told him to do, but I got sicker every day. I got so thin they continued to call me "Bones."

It had taken my father about a year to visit these priests, gather the images for his sanctuary, and complete his task. When my mother saw all that was happening, she said, "Listen, I'm going to go back to what I believe. My family did everything by praying to God first," she said. "If you want to, you can go out there and worship all kinds of spirits, but I will do it my way." So even though my mother allowed my father to follow his way of thinking to resolve our family issues, she believed in God.

Chapter 17

Christianity in Haiti

My current understanding dictates that some of Haiti's population did not have a proper account of the gospel of Christ, particularly from the Catholic church. Creole's daily language and most Bibles were in Latin or French.

There was a statue of the Virgin Mary in the adjacent church. That was the hospital where I was born. My mother bought clothes in blue and white and a bonnet to dress me. Then she put a blanket in front of the statue and put me on the rug. She prayed for me for days and days and days.

So, our home had two forces: my mother praying to God and my father praying to the spirits.

At one point, my father found a voodoo priest who wanted to come to our house to live with us. My parents provided him with a bed. He spent hours and hours performing different kinds of ceremonies, using all sorts of potions. Some relatives came to the house and sang voodoo songs. Everyone was trying to cure me.

One day the voodoo priest became a host to a spirit, and he proclaimed that this was the only way he could liberate me from my illness. The priest/spirit informed my parents that the magic world's spirits had chosen me to become a voodoo priest even before I was born. My father had to give my soul away, and my father agreed. "OK, I accept; my son will be a voodoo priest," he said.

My mother and father kept praying and praying, each in their way according to their personal beliefs, and one day I started to eat. Then, when I was sick, my mother said that my stools would come out in different colors even though I would not eat anything or take any medicine.

My parents believed I had an evil spirit around me all the time, but I guess I lacked medical attention.

Finally, my parents went to another medical doctor. "Little lady and young man," he said. "I give your son a couple of months to live, and there is nothing you can do."

May would weep so profoundly and leave me on her bed. We did not have a crib, and I slept in the same bed as my mother and father. They would lay me on the couch and go about their work.

One day to their amazement, I got up and started to talk. IT RELIEVED THEM when I finally learned to speak and asked for food. I had spent two years struggling for my life, and the change was the beginning of my healing.

After they believed I had become the chosen person, my father kept everything the voodoo priests had told him to have. He decorated this shrine in every apartment we moved to and found a corner to put the items that comprised his sanctuary.

He always had his little shrine box in one corner of the house. Every Tuesday and Thursday, he would light candles in front of the TV. Once a year, he would invite a family member to come over and sing songs until the spirits took ownership of his body.

As the days went by, I did get better. To this day, I do not believe my dad building a shrine is what cured me. In later chapters, I will explain my encounter with God, my contact with God's knowledge, and what God has done for me.

Throughout this book, I use the word spirit of how my parents and the Haitian culture have explained it. In Haiti, they use the word "Loa. The English dictionary defines the phrase as a supernatural, incorporeal creature, particularly one who inhabits a location, object, or character. Some people may even use it to denote a fairy, sprite, elf, angel, or demon. My beliefs would classify it as wicked or demon spirits.

In the Haitian cultural environment or beliefs, there are two types of spirits: The one that provides protection just like an angel and inflicts harm like a demon. Worshipers believe the supernatural nature of a traditional spirit invocation involves calling ancestors who have passed away.

Since I provided somewhat detailed info regarding the world of Voodooism, I think I should establish equilibrium by providing you with some references to what the Bible teaches:

Leviticus 19:31: "Do not turn to mediums or necromancers; do not seek them out and make yourselves unclean by them: I am the Lord your God.

Isaiah 8:19: And when they say to you, "Inquire of the mediums and the necromancers who chirp and mutter," should not a people inquire of their God? Should they ask of the dead-on behalf of the living?

Leviticus 20:6: "And the soul that turned after such as have familiar spirits, and after wizards, to go astray after them, I will even set my face against that soul and cut him off from among his people."

Chapter 18

Shrine and Rituals

Because of his experience with the ill child, my father took Andre Dante's advice seriously. He customarily performed ceremonial activities on Christmas Eve or between October and November 2nd to commemorate "Fet Gede" or "Feast of the Dead." It celebrates Baron Samedi, the Vondon God of Death and father of the spirit of the dead; The tradition remained till his death.

During those days, I always felt uncomfortable around Christmas Eve and Halloween.

I knew I did not want to participate in the party that was going to come. When the celebration would take place, I always worked hard to find an alternate location to distract myself. These routines had an emotional influence on how I perceive life.

When the time came, my father would enlist the help of his family members to execute religious ceremonies to summon the ghosts of his ancestors who had died. Worshiping deities represented by like Catholic saints were part of the ceremonies. Most households have a shrine devoted to the saints, and ours did.

My father and his saints had their shrines in the corner of his room. The shrine has representations of all the saints that my father considers to be protective shields. My mother and children were not allowed to stay.

Each chosen spirit is represented by a framed photo, with one or more accouterments or symbols next to each image. Worshipers gave distinct titles to each soul that took possession of a person's body throughout the worship ceremony. They make sacrifices and pray to various spirits based on the action they are about to conduct.

Agwe, if he is the ghost, has a short beard and gray hair. He is tall, and participants regarded him as the ocean's monarch. Worshipers pray to him when traveling by water, believing that their fidelity and allegiance to him will guide them safely; the contrary may cause them to disappear amid the ocean. Worshippers identified the spirit as St. Ulrich, whose emblems include boats with paddles and fish. Champagne, white sheep, or white chicken are standard offerings.

Worshippers think that if the spirit is Zaka, he resides in the fields and considers the land his dominion. He is the harvest guardian, and his popularity is extremely high since farmers rely on him to protect their harvests. He dislikes those who steal and dislikes people who talk a lot. He has a crimson handkerchief in his pocket to wipe away sweat from the blazing heat. A little reptile, a pipe, and a machete are his symbol. He is comparable to Sts. Andre and Isidore.

When the ghost is Baron Samedi, people think he spends much of his time in the cemetery and must wear very dark spectacles when not in his world. He occasionally appears among the living, dressed as a sick beggar in ragged clothing, but most of the time, he wears a black coat with tails and a top hat, and he carries a cane with a skull for a handle. He enjoys using hot peppers and spices in his cocktails; some estimate he uses twenty different herbs. Some believe he knows everything there is to know about humanity. Believers believe he resembles St. Andrew.

If the spirit is Damballa, he generally carries a stick adorned with a golden coiled serpent and a man's head, and his wife is known as Ayada Wedo. That ghost is an elderly guy with a long white beard. People frequently refer to him and his female companion simultaneously; therefore, the combined name represents fertility. Some think he is the creator and link his female companion to the Immaculate Conception of the Virgin Mary. Her colors are blue and white, and her emblem is a rainbow. The followers know that pleasure and money are the central motivation for getting excited when the ghost appears. The spirits appreciate the cotton and silk tree. They are looking for white foods like cauliflower, milk, maize, chicken, and rice. They expect their followers to be devout believers.

If the spirit says her name is Elzili Dantor, she is a beautiful mother who loves her children. She protects them like a black panther would protect her cubs. She prefers the colors blue, red, and black. She requires fried pork and black pigs and likes rum and cigarettes. Her deity is the spirit of motherhood, and her symbol is a heart with a knife. She is known for her courage. Some believe she was there during the Haitian Revolution against the French, at least in mind.

Elzili Freda is another female spirit that shows up sometimes. She is one of the most beautiful and graceful of all souls. Her exquisite appearance causes men to fall for her quickly. She represents fertility and has love relations with other entities. She is mixed-race with long hair and wears elegant white, red, or pink gowns. She loves perfumes and other fragrances; her symbols are hearts and a mirror.

They also feature a spirit named Gran Brijit. She is supposedly married to Baron Samedi, and these two do not get along. She is private, often resides in solitude, and has a strong personality. She better understands mortal pleas than her husband, perhaps the source of their disagreement. She does not like alcohol and prefers black coffee and dark chocolate, and she plays a significant role in ruling the paradise realm of the departed. She resembles St. Catherine, St. Teresa, or St. Bridget; Her favorite colors are purple and black. Her worshipers seek her advice often.

Another spirit named Gran Bois, or Big Tree, looks like a tree due to his connection with the forest. People see him as half a tree and half a man, and they usually ask permission from him before cutting down a tree. He holds the secrets of all things related to herbs and plants, and he has branches like a tree coming out of his body that represent his hands and feet, which run into the ground like roots. Finally, Haiti has a tree called the mapou (its likeness is in the movie Avatar as the "home tree"), and the mapou is his favorite tree. He is mighty. He prefers leaves, peanut cake, cassava bread, tobacco, and cornmeal. His symbols are wood and roots.

If the spirit is La Sirene, she is one of the most enchanting, beautiful, and sexy female spirits. That deity lives in the ocean, and people associate her with seduction, good fortune, and prosperity. She is often seen in the sea combing her long hair and considering a mirror, and worshipers believe she has neither arms nor clothing. She prefers perfume, white wine, and mirrors; her symbols are combs, shells, and trumpets. Worshipers usually announce her arrival by blowing into a seashell.

Legba is responsible for opening the gate to all the other spirits. Worshipers usually call on him first. He walks with a cane, and people often invoke him when encountering a crossroads. He smokes and drinks frequently. Catholics associate him with St. Peter, Lazarus, and St. Anthony. His symbols are keys, crosses, walking sticks, or an older man in tatters.

Even though there are more, I have chosen to describe these entities, so you can imagine the inner core of what I experienced as a child. The services are like visiting a seance with a voodoo priest without the presence of cards to reveal trials in someone's life.

The celebration starts with participants surrounding one person the spirits will use as hosts. Most services involve members of one family and close relatives. In our household, my father always took the role of a host.

Once all participants are present, I remember my dad spending some time praying in front of the shrine. He would first pray to the Almighty God for permission to invoke the spirits. Without such authorization, he believed the deity would not be able to hear him.

After the prayer, my dad rings a tiny bell and takes a sip of clairin in his mouth. Clairin is an alcoholic drink like tequila, but probably more vital. He spits it out, sprinkles somebody with it, or sprays it all over the room. One could hear the bell resonate randomly as the service continued. Next, he lights out some candles and places them strategically around the house. My Dad took a cup of water and sprinkled it in front of the house. He pulls out a machete and smacks it against each room corner.

When I saw my dad making noises with the sword slapping it on different house walls, it was a terrifying demonstration to witness. He might dance for a while. He kneels and stays in a trance for an extended period, sometimes for an hour or more. When he opens his eyes, his voice sounds much different than his own, and he suddenly becomes the spirit that possesses him.

If a knight takes control of my dad, described as riding a horse trying to cross a lake of fire, participants treat it as hostile. I saw my dad's eyes turn red, and his hair stood out, and he started to talk and tell people who he was and how many legions he had behind him. After a few demonstrations of some odd behaviors, the host, under the spirit's control, would begin to instruct other observers regarding the specific expectation of what they need to do to please the deity in session.

I heard participants talking and getting ready to have the spirits ride them. They talk about riding since the deity refers to them as horses.

Worshipers treat spirits just like a close member of the family. Every morning they feed coffee to the deity by dropping a few drops on the ground to express sharing.

As the ceremony continues, participants sit down just like any religious gathering. They sing folkloric songs. The master of the service asks a particular spirit to come over a person, and the person remains still until the deity arrives.

When the spirit appears, the new host starts to quiver like someone experiencing an episode of epilepsy. He takes a sip of the clairin and makes a thunderous noise, jumping in the air. The host drops like somebody with an electric shock—as the jumping continues, sometimes doing somersaults and falling on the floor. These actions were hard to witness; there were times when I thought a person would get hurt, and I never saw anyone get hurt, as far as I can recall.

After the new host falls, the master of the ceremony approaches them and calms them down.

After the new spirit surfaces, He would sometimes ask where he is and what is the place's name. Then, he would talk to different people and shake their hands. Then, after shaking as many hands as he could, he would tell them about himself.

Participants are usually curious and anxious to hear about what will happen to them. Therefore, participants want to know the following:

- Is a member of the family going to get sick?
- Is something terrible going to happen in the next few months?
- What is the name of the following spirit?
- Is the next Spirit hostile or docile?

Participants would line up and ask questions about each of them. Sometimes with cigars and cane in hand, the host/spirit answered questions believers had previously prepared.

For instance, some of the questions might relate to business. If they start a business, they ask the spirit for advice regarding the best way to complete the task.

The people at the seance instructed the host on what the Spirit gave them. The spirit would tell them things like: "Before you start your business, you should go and feed some members of your family who died a long time ago, and you should go and purchase certain food for them and feed them. After doing that, you can come back and start a new business. Everything is going to be alright. Sometimes the spirit would have specific instructions for the host, and the other members of the family would tell him, "Hey, spirit so-and-so was here, or Mr. Damballa was there, or Mrs. Guede was there," and he would say, "Oh, is that right?" The host does not remember what happened to them when the seance is over.

They treat their deities like they are part of their family, an actual living person. If the person doesn't like the instructions, sometimes he gets mad, saying, "Hey, I don't want to do what the spirit prescribed. It is fascinating to watch.

After all this work, the host would get very tired, and he goes to sleep before they can resume the day or the next, just like nothing ever happened.

Another peculiar portion of these ceremonies involves a spirit called Guede. Guede is a woman's spirit, and she is extremely hostile. She likes lots of hot peppers, jalapeno, red, green, and black peppers mixed with clairin; exceptional food. Only a woman can be a host to Guede.

The host prepares a unique concoction for the spirit throughout the year. Once a year, around Halloween or the day of the dead, a host would summon Guede. She would gather alcohol and peppers, put them in a jar, seal the pot, and bury them in the ground. She would cross over to the spot where she hid it and light a candle next. When the time comes, she pulls out the jar, which the Guede consumes. The potion stays there for an entire year.

During the ceremony, Guede would come out and ask for her potion. Although this is a boiling potion with alcohol and peppers, the host doesn't feel anything. The host feeds Guede through her mouth and even through her vagina.

They do not let children watch this type of ceremony due to the feeding process, the host having to swear a lot, and the excessive use of filthy language.

The host feels obligated to perform this ritual to please Guede for fear of future punishment.

There is a belief that they feed the dead and do not like salt. Some have gone to the extreme of believing salt would turn them into zombies that can hurt the living. When sacrifice time comes, my mother cooks a lot of food, mostly rice without salt.

After the seance is over in the morning, the family distributes the food among the children.

A story that says a long time ago was a man who did not believe that when these people prepared the food, they would give it to a particular spirit. When they cooked the traditional chicken meal, they put the chicken on top of a tree, and this man ate it. The next day they found him dead.

Chapter 19

My Parents' Wedding

My father had his own house, a five-room home with three bedrooms, a living room, and a dining room. My father wanted to keep the promise of marrying my mother, and I was nine years of age when that occurred. After much preparation, they had a gorgeous wedding.

My father started to make a lot more money because he had his shop, but the government built more roads. He received additional work. His job was to change trailers imported from the United States into vehicles. The population used these containers to travel from the cities to the suburbs. It would take him a week or two weeks to make one truck. This work allowed him to earn between a thousand to two thousand dollars for each job. That was a lot of money for us.

He felt a little more comfortable, and we started seeing things differently. We grew up more relaxed and acquired enough money to build our house.

Since things were going very well for him, he felt it was time to marry my mother, but he could not wed the spirits unless he married my mother first. Anyway, he kept his promise, and they had a lovely wedding. The wedding was in a Catholic church far from where we lived. I was a little bit confused then, and the reason I was confused because they had gone to church once a week for almost a year to get ready for that wedding. I thought they were going to change things.

But things did not turn out because my parents were married. We already had five children in the house and participated in the wedding. It was a lovely wedding, and They did not use voodoo during that ritual. The time was also coming for my father to marry the spirits.

Chapter 20

Wedding with the Spirits

One day, he informed my mother that he had to marry two spirits after marrying her. The black Virgin Mary is one of the spirits, while the white Virgin Mary is another. Performing a ritual with these spirits would purify him and give him more power in the spirit realm. When these spirits take over someone's body, they encourage my father to marry them. As a result, he did. My parents assembled a small group of close relatives and had a spirit wedding ceremony. They were both married.

My father had a room in our house dedicated to these ladies. He slept there on Tuesdays and Thursdays to ensure he was close to the black Virgin Mary and the white virgin. He wore a different ring each day to represent his devotion to each.

When I saw this, I wanted to abscond away. However, this was my home, and too young to make any practical decision to go anywhere else. The situation has become complex, and I was unsure how I could adapt or live with this type of environment.

Chapter 21

Sister's Illness

Despite the city's traditional and contemporary physicians and clinics, many licensed and nonlicensed health providers endorsed alternative medicine. Some of them were part-time Doulas who occasionally assisted pregnant women in giving birth while also dabbling in other types of illness cures. There was one such person who affected our lives. We called her Adriana. We never thought she would get involved in what would happen next. She has always been a simple woman with whom our family shared a meal. On multiple occasions, she would stop by to update my mom or my dad on the countryside town gossip. Her politeness and sweet mannerism would easily be confused as someone with your best interest at heart.

When my sister Veronica woke up one day, she informed us that she had stepped on an unusual object. Maybe she wasn't paying attention to where she was going, or someone strategically placed the item where she would come in contact with her body. Somehow, we would never know. The next day, we noticed one of her feet started to swell.

Subsequently, she couldn't walk comfortably and had to lie down after a few steps. She couldn't complete a full day of work or school without complaining about the severity of her pain. She returned home after barely starting a day of work. That was the beginning of a horrendous string of sick days for her. She never wore high-heeled shoes; therefore, it couldn't be a stress fracture, plantar fasciitis, or Achilles tendinitis. Doctors who have seen her foot determined there were no puncture wounds, injuries to ligaments, or ruptured tendons in her heels. They couldn't find any sprains or broken bones.

At the time of the incident, she weighed between 170 to 180 pounds. Gradually, it became much more challenging for her to walk with this type of injury, so she had to stay in the hospital for a week. We took her to the doctor, who took X-rays of her feet. The roentgenograms revealed nothing amiss with her. The physicians had to repeat different procedures to ensure they did not miss anything serious.

Day after day, my sister's toes kept swelling hard and were heavy, and she needed help to prop her foot up to get a certain amount of relief. Physicians couldn't figure out why they did not find any infection.

We began to suspect that someone was superstitiously harming her. Every time we prepared to go to the hospital, whether by coincidence or not, the swelling seemed to go down. My parents had convinced themselves that she had experienced something otherworldly. Consequently, my father called Adriana and others he felt could be familiar with a similar disease. Adriana was the most active participant in uncovering what was happening among those he contacted. Despite his trust in Adriana, he traveled to the provinces, as he typically did when events shook his faith. His goal was to protect his children, especially when one of us became sick. He wants us to be well, be our best, and be able to play around in the yard and go to school without any issues.

Meanwhile, Adriana and other alternative physicians would come over and attempt various recognized therapies, but nothing changed; she did not get well. I discovered that merging voodoo with protestant worship did not work well for us.

I needed to figure out what was bothering my sister. I focused on confronting similar illnesses and investigating if the Bible had a mystery cure. As my trust in God strengthened, I read the Bible more regularly.

I became even more concerned when I read 2 Chronicles 16:12.

"In the thirty-ninth year of his reign, Asa became diseased in his feet. His disease was severe, yet even in his disease, he did not seek the Lord, but the physicians."

I kept saying to myself that God would eventually help. He was with me and always gave me protection because He knew my heart; I did not want to serve or practice the religion of my parents. He knew that even though they told me one time that the deities had chosen me and, yes, God chose me, God selected me to become His servant, not a servant of spirits who did not die on the cross for me.

Throughout this time, I was a frequent attendee of the Seventh-day Adventist Church. After reading James 5:14, *"Is anyone among you sick? Then he must call for the church's elders, who are to pray over him, anointing him with oil in the name of the Lord."*

Consequently, I invited some of my fellow worshippers to come over and pray for her regularly.

As the days went by, my sister would cry, appear to be hallucinating, not getting enough sleep, and feel that somebody was holding her feet down all the time. My father brought different people over to cure her, but none of these people could do anything. Even though she started going to church with me, her faith wavered. She wanted to get healed and did not care what to do to get treated.

On a specific day, Adriana came to the house with a promise to cure her. She began preparing to perform a mystical ceremony. When she arrived, I was nowhere near participating; I was in church, and on my way back, I got to the door and saw candles at the gate. I knew something was going on inside. I started to shiver, got goosebumps, and my hair stood on end; I felt uncomfortable going inside. As

I paced the corridor that would take me to the house, I had numerous thoughts on what I should say if someone attempted to approach me for conversation. Every so often, I would go in if I needed something from inside, but I never wanted to contribute or share whatever they were concocting in their private room. On many occasions before, whenever I saw similar situations, I would go far away to be alone or pray if possible.

When I finally decided to go inside for good, I carefully tiptoed until I reached my destination. As I sneaked to get a peak of what was going on, I thought no one could not see me. I was too far away from the room where Adriana was operating her little tricks to distract them. For some unexplainable reason, Adriana knew I was there, and I heard her say: "Hey, somebody is in there who is not supposed to be there, you'd better get that person out, or I will not be able to perform what is necessary."

Adriana insisted I stay away. Other people were working with her, and the people involved got me out. After the ceremony, I am not sure what exactly she did; I noticed my sister's feet came down flat, I asked what happened, and she showed us that she had pulled out five little lizards from her feet. Deep down, I knew it was some tricks that charlatans play on naïve audiences.

I can't tell you what type of shenanigans she pulled that day. I saw the dead lizards on the floor and refused to believe they were on her feet, but my sister said she knew they were there because she felt something crawling on her feet.

My belief in God and other things that humanity has persuaded others to accept as reality has grown more extensive. Many individuals believe in God or other deities simply because of fear. Regardless of the degree of knowledge, they have acquired over the years, and those curious will go to tremendous lengths to read the Bible or the Koran. Their surroundings had trained them to do so, and they accepted it intuitively.

I heard a tale of a man who couldn't read but desperately wanted to preach the gospel, so he studied the life of Christ until he knew it by memory. He memorized the Bible by listening to biblical recordings. He was a Seventh-day Adventist who used colored crayons to label the New Testament by theme. He would emphasize everything concerning the resurrection and Christ in one color, everything about the Sabbath in a different hue, the spirits in gray, and so on. He had at least ten distinct subjects, each of which was a different hue. He has highlighted the whole New Testament in various shades. He remembered biblical texts based on colors with the aid of others.

The process allowed him to talk to people. Even though he could not read, he would show the scriptures, and the person would read them to him. They would understand, and he could bring many people to Jesus Christ in this way. I thought that was beautiful. No matter how they serve people, they have a chance and freedom to worship God.

After the incident with my sister's foot, she started religiously going to church. Even today, I believe she has become more dedicated than I ever was.

Chapter 22

My Religious Believes

The narrative in the news and social media involving religious beliefs in Haiti affects how people characterize its history. Sometimes I wonder whether I become trapped in the same way of thinking even after living nearly fifty years in the United States.

The prevailing storyline is inaccurate. We are not a monolithic society. Not everyone born in Haiti feels, believes, or thinks the same way.

In truth, today's statistics show that fifty-two percent of Haitians are Protestant, Episcopalian, Jehovah's witnesses Methodist, or Seventh-day Adventist. Thirty-five percent follow Catholicism. Eleven percent do not affiliate themselves with beliefs, and only two percent publicly practice voodooism.

As a young man, I knew I had a choice to think independently regardless of all the noises surrounding me. In my inner thoughts, I believed, as I have often heard, that God has a plan tailored just for me.

My mother has done an excellent job of steering me toward church teachings rather than ancestral beliefs. She would talk to me and tell me, "Son, I know you will be a priest or a pastor someday, no matter what happens. I know you will not be a voodoo priest; I know you will be a Catholic or evangelical priest." That was inspiring because I needed to hear that even though I had no desire to become a priest—her encouragement to guide me away from voodooism showed me the right direction.

As peristil or altars decorated with images of Jesus, Marie, Joseph, and other saints often filled home and church temples, I needed the correct strength to filter my thinking.

As my attendance in the church became more frequent, my perception of God's existence evolved tremendously. That was true then and is true to my ever-changing personality. Family members on my mother's side and fellow Christians have helped me to learn about God's desires.

You will overcome adversities if you have a strong anchor regarding right and wrong. For example, even though I grew up around people who smoked incessantly and over-consumed alcohol, I never wanted to emulate them. Maybe God taught me that a corrupted environment doesn't have to overpower my thinking. I learned that temptations could come in every shape and form.

Every time I wanted or needed something, I cultivated the habit of secretly kneeling and praying until God would answer my prayers. If I thought for a moment I was not getting the desired answer; I was not disappointed. My faith did not waiver because of the idea planted in my head that God has a plan. Not everything you ask is good for you.

Most of the time, I prayed to God, and He responded. I prayed to the Lord to make me different. Perhaps the Lord intended me to feel distinct about myself for this reason.

The yearly state examination is a great example. The government administers an education competence assessment, and students from all schools gather in one room to get an evaluation and take a challenging test that lasts for hours. This test is significant for all young men who need a successful future. Without such accomplishment, a shameful shadow follows you wherever you go.

Students often take a final state exam in their senior year of high school. Sometimes, for some of these students, the examination is repeated, meaning they were unsuccessful in prior years. The psychological tension is usually high. Unfortunately, I did not attend a school with a reputation for success.

I wanted to succeed. I studied very hard while praying simultaneously. The hope of me not having to add my name to the failure list was putting a lot of pressure on me and my parents. The day came, and I participated in each examination like I had an army of angels escorting me. We had to wait at least two weeks before they would announce the winner over an FM radio station.

The above example is not unusual; life continuously puts my beliefs to the test—every problem I face puts my faith to the test. That afternoon, a group gathered around a tiny radio to hear names read aloud in alphabetical order. When they got to the B area, I could hear shouts as they called out my name.

Religious Views in Haiti

The Pew Research Center released the following data on religious views in Haiti in 2010. Roman Catholicism had 56.8%, while Protestantism had 29.6%. Furthermore, 10.6% of the population declared no religion, while 3% adhered to faiths other than Catholicism and Protestantism.

Voodooism is a universally accepted syncretic religion. The idea blended West African notions of enslaved Africans. It has a beautiful flare for Catholicism and specific Native American threads; Cuban Santera shares the same value system.

The same is true in Haitian history, and Christianity reigns supreme. Syncretism has some adjustments and impacts in specific conditions.

According to the 2015 CIA World Factbook, Roman Catholicism accounts for 80% of the population. The French influence was crucial in maintaining Catholic dominance.

When Pope John Paul II visited Haiti in 1983, he delivered an eloquent address. Many thought the Pope's address significantly influenced Haiti's Catholic bureaucracy, contributing to Jean Claude Duvalier's resignation in 1986. Roman Catholicism has long been popular in Haiti and Latin America, and until 1987, the Haitian government incorporated Catholicism into its constitution.

The Catholic Church has ten dioceses in two provinces, with around 251 locations and over 1500 Christian rural communities. There are almost 400 priests and 300 seminarians. Missionary priests are pretty famous, and numerous belong to other denominations.

Meanwhile, Protestants account for about 16% of the population, Seventh-Day Adventists for 1%, Baptists for 4%, Pentecostals for 4%, and other organizations for 1%. In 2017, the church reported 46 churches and over 22,300 members in Haiti. Les Cayes, Saint-Marc, and Gonaves are all districts of the capital area.

In May of 1980, The Mormons commenced activities on the island. In September 2012, the ministry created the third and fourth Haitian stakes.

The Holy Trinity Cathedral, or Cathédrale Sainte Trinité in French, has known destruction six times, including the 2010 earthquake.

The Episcopal Church has members throughout the provincial regions of Haiti. It is an Anglican Communion diocese and a member of the United States Episcopal Church's Second Province. As of 2022, the Episcopal Church had

1,678,157 members, most of whom lived in the United States. I traced my mother's heritage back to that group.

Jewish culture has existed for a long time; they came to the Dominican Republic during the early colonial days. Despite their difficulties in other regions of the country, Haiti welcomed them freely at the time.

They were businessmen and members of the French Catholic group. Several groups moved to Haiti, notably Ashkenazi Jews fleeing Hitler's Germany in the 1940s.

Abdu'l-Bahá leads the Bahá' Faith. This religion began to spread throughout the Caribbean Island countries. In 1927, Leonora Armstrong visited Haiti, and others followed in 1937. In 1942, they founded the first Bahá' Local Spiritual Assembly in Haiti.

Voodoo encompasses several traditions and religious elements; these values may have come from Africa, Europe, and indigenous Taíno. The practice of the New World Afro-diasporic religion of voodoo exists in Haiti. It is like other Latin American syncretist movements, such as the Cuban Santería. The voodoo faith is widespread in rural parts of the country, partly due to its negative stigmas. During Lent season, voodoo societies have carnivals and musical groups for an annual jubilee called Rara and fulfill religious obligations in local spaces such as streams, rivers, and trees.

According to the CIA World Factbook, about 50% of the population practices voodoo. Many do not believe this figure because there is an overlap with the practice of Roman Catholicism and other religious faiths. Those who are members of the Protestants society are less prone to follow the beliefs of voodooism, and their church treats voodooism as diabolical.

Haiti has a tiny population that believes in the Muslim faith. They reside in the capital of Port-au-Prince, and some live in Cap-Haitian and other surrounding communities. Many Muslims came to the island as enslaved people.

In 2000, Nawoon Marcellus became the first Muslim elected to the Chamber of Deputies of Haiti. He was a member of Fanmi Lavalas from Saint-Raphaël.

Chapter 23

Political Exposure

National Pride

Every year on May 22nd, volunteers from nearby towns of Port-au-Prince leave their homes to visit the national palace. It didn't matter if they wanted to, as the order came straight from their commander-in-chief. The government dispatched vehicles and camionettes (fancy-dressed buses or pickup trucks used as accessible taxis) into the countryside to force every 'volunteer' to come to the capital. It was a source of tremendous pleasure to be a member of the Tonton Macoute, and the organization put on large exhibitions on significant occasions regularly.

They compelled schoolchildren, including myself, to take part in this celebration. I recall standing in line with the rest of my classmates and marching for hours from my school to the palace courtyard without food or drink. Trucks and camionettes full of Tonton Macoute would pass by as we walked, generally chanting Duvalier's theme tunes. When we arrived, we would form a line with students from all the other schools, everyone wearing their school uniform, and sing songs and recite the Pledge that Duvalier had prepared for pupils to repeat every morning.

"Je jure devant Dieu et devant la nation, d'en être le gardien intraitable et farouche. Qu'il flotte désormais dans l'azur. Pour rappeler à tous les Haïtiens les prouesses de nos sublimes martyrs. de la Crête à Pierrot, de la Butte Charrier et de Vertières qui se sont immortalisés, sous les boulets et la mitraille, pour nous créer une patrie, où le nègre haitien, se sent réellement souverain et libre"

In English: "I swear before God and the nation; to be the intractable and fierce guardian that would at this moment floats in the sky. To remind all Haitians of the sublime achievements of our martyrs, of Crete Pierrot of the Butte Charrier and Vertières whom we admire for their sacrifices, as bullets and shrapnel, for us to create a country where the Haitian Negro feels truly sovereign and free."

I was proud at the time that I had distant cousins in the volunteer army who were prominent and openly carried weaponry they might use to help Papa Doc. The Tonton Macoutes were well-liked by specific sectors of the population. My father worked with several so-called Tonto Macoute, or National Security troops. Despite this, he never considered joining them. It took me years to understand why: although many individuals were delighted to be Boogeymen, many others believed the Tonton Macoute as victims, sad souls corrupted and warped by the very system they swore to preserve.

This tradition was so constant and efficient that many people volunteered to join the Tonton Macoute in exchange for different benefits. Among these benefits was free transportation to the capital, where they planned to settle and live! Unfortunately, the departure affected farming communities in the island's most isolated areas. Their communities were suddenly underpopulated; Port-au-Prince, on the other hand, was tremendously overpopulated. The people had fewer food crops after several years of this trend and a shortage of agricultural finance. Farmers were not producing enough food to meet domestic demand as the population grew. As a result, Haiti had to import a significant portion of its agricultural commodities.

Chapter 24

Mother Nature's impact

Hurricane Flora

From September 30th to October 8th, 1963, hurricane Flora left its destructive path in Haiti. For nine hours, during one of those days, Haiti was pounded with torrential rain and wind up to 140 miles per hour, some newspapers reported. This mother nature of events isolated the country from the rest of the world. This hurricane took more than 7,200 lives and left thousands of people homeless in Cuba, the Dominican Republic, and Haiti. All the stores had closed signs. No one could go outside, and the flood started to come.

I remember my mom and dad skirmishing to keep us from drowning because the floods have risen to an almost tree-top level in some areas. "Where is your sister," my mother asked me. "She is still outside playing in the rain," I said. "Do you want to die, little girl? Get in here," she said out loud to my sister. "Take the kid's mattress, put them on top of the table, and it is higher than the bed," she argued with dad. "It does not matter; the water is coming too fast; get the kids on top of the table instead.

A thumping noise suddenly came, and the front door swung open as the wind threw a wave of rainwater over everything inside. I looked at my mother, her hair, face, and clothes soaked with water. "Don't move, stay on top of the table, hang on tight to your sister, give me the baby, no, give me the baby," they argued. The wind came again; my younger brother fell into the water. "Grab him quick, so he does not drown," my mother said. We stayed at the table for a long time until it was over. At night, we lit the gas lamp so that we could see. The first night after the flood, we kids slept while our parents stayed up to watch us.

Tree leaves and broken branches covered the area as a strong wind similar to a tornado had just run through a misfortunate town during the fall season. The deluge from the hurricane carried garbage from the streets and the sewer inside our home. The stench of dead rats and outdoor toilets invaded the air.

The water had destroyed most of our bedding. In Port-au-Prince, people built houses with cement blocks and corrugated tin roofs. One by one, we watched the wind lifting the tin sheets as nails became no longer stable to hold them in place. People see their neighbors in a worse situation than they were and come over to help to the best of their abilities.

Two by four pieces of wood rattled underneath and flew at 25 miles per hour in the air. I remember electrical wires hanging down from poles and spark illuminating the ground here and there. Innocent bystanders would pick them up, so they could go through. Some got electrocuted, and some got around without incident. I remember one gentleman that lived next door to us. The intense force of the wind instantly killed him with a sheet metal that hit him in the neck. After it was all over, we could not afford to buy new furniture. Our parents had to go through a long process of salvaging whatever we could to survive.

Haitian Farmers watched in horror as the rain turned into rivers; the crops washed into the ocean with the soil; they worked hard to protect them for the next harvest. Street merchants could no longer sell their merchandise because they were busy trying to salvage the unspoiled little. People did not know where to go to buy anything.

The aftermath of the hurricane was just as sad as the events themselves. People took a long time to recover, and everyone experienced the same loss. Suddenly, people had to struggle to clean their houses. After the rain had ceased and the water receded, each house had at least two to four feet of mud inside.

Many houses no longer had a roof. Neighbors brought shovels to help in the removal of dirt. Mattresses had water in them and started to smell bad. Instead of throwing them away, people would squeeze the water out of them and spread them outside in the sun to dry. "We cannot use this again; just throw them away; I would rather sleep on the floor," my mom argued with my dad.

"Fine, where will we find another one? The mattresses from the store also have damage. The best option is to wash the sheets clean after removing the mud. Meanwhile, we are going to sleep on the floor."

Life inside and outside was miserable, to say the least, for at least a week after the hurricane. Then, the price of everything got skyrocketed.

Our house was just a few blocks from the railroad. The train that ran through came from Leogane, a small-town west of Port-au-Prince. It carried sugar cane. Brave kids would hear the train coming and race on each train's side. They would pull loose stems of sugar cane plants and distribute them around the area. The sugar kept them going until other things became available. It was a dangerous practice that some people were grateful for when the train came. Occasionally, an unfortunate youngster would get caught and get run over. In either case, they would either get killed or lose a limb.

Day by day, life was a struggle wherever you looked. The experience of seeing gunshots in school at an early age has undoubtedly left some emotional scars on me. I quickly realize the intimidation of others with power is not unique, no matter where you live. I have seen mother nature tear through belongings and worldly materials we hold dear. This exposure helped me understand what is essential to life.

You probably heard this quote before: "The problem is not the problem." Your attitude about the issue can make all the difference in the world. Life is full of surprises, and it will always be a roller-coaster. The downhill moments are necessary periods designed to shape your character so that you can enjoy the pinnacle moments better.

Natural disasters, political turmoil, and religious and day-to-day emotional challenges exist so you can know what to do to survive when facing your life problems.

Chapter 25

Understanding the Culture

Whether you were born in Haiti or not, it has been challenging to characterize the country in recent decades without using the phrase "the poorest nation in the Western Hemisphere." However, whether fair or not, the penalty does not honor the millions of individuals who fought tirelessly to make a difference.

Are the people of Haiti cursed?

A person's personal views determine the answer to the question. As I dug through history to discover the answer to that question, I couldn't help but notice the numerous institutions that contributed to Haiti's current state. It was not my intention to have this book pointing fingers at others. However, it will assist you, the reader, in comprehending many parts of Haiti's historical anatomy.

People used to refer to Haiti as the "Jewel of the Caribbean" for a long time. Despite the obstacles, its people remain proud. They thrive daily with a sense of fulfillment that does not come from material stuff.

Haitians are happy to be the world's second free nation, behind the United States.

If we analyze the circumstances that led to Haiti's independence, we will agree that it might have originated from Hollywood's warped imagination. In

1751, lawmakers passed the first legislation degrading the position of the black community.

People who used to be free found themselves in situations where their oppressors treated them as if they were the lowest object in the world - they worked as unpaid servants for foreign European invaders. They stared in horror as their masters dined, enjoying the fruits of their work, while their bodies were still aching from the punishment they 'earned' the night before for allegedly misbehaving.

Those who believed in the Supreme Being prayed for the ability to control their anger while they endured strange circumstances daily.

In 1791, France's government, which controlled the majority of Haiti, attempted to temper rising rage by awarding citizenship to some of the wealthiest enslaved people. Nonetheless, the white plantation owners refused to submit to the French government's directives. When the enslaved people learned of the betrayal, a northern voodoo priest named Dutty Boukman convened a religious assembly, and the enslaved people rose immediately and violently.

They destroyed approximately 200 sugar, coffee, and indigo crops within a season. They had control of the northern portion of the island within a year.

In a panic at the end of 1792, France declared all province freemen citizens. This action did not benefit the enslaved people, but it irritated Britain and Spain, who sought to take over France's territories.

The white plantation owners of Haiti sided with Britain, while the Spanish section of Hispaniola, now known as the Dominican Republic, was connected with the rebel enslaved people. The consequence was a three-way battle between French soldiers and the French government, plantation owners and British supporters, and enslaved people with the assistance of Spain.

The French army had been repeatedly beaten and pushed practically into hiding by August 1793. France's presence in the region remained in existence, though in a smaller number. Out of desperation, France declared all enslaved people free, firmly unifying the French and slave-Spanish sides of the conflict against the British and the plantation owners. The French government followed the model of liberty provided by the American Revolution: "universal liberty," they termed it.

Of course, the conflict had not ended. Nonetheless, the Declaration of Liberty introduced a new, powerful player to the field: Toussaint Louverture, a self-educated enslaved person and skilled tactician who first fought for the Spanish, swiftly joined France and took his army with him. France failed to recognize that Louverture desired autonomy rather than restoring the enslaved people to French domination.

The Spanish were forced back to their territories under his command, and Louverture's troops regularly beat Britain until they stopped attacking. Finally, in 1801, Louverture drafted a constitution fashioned after the American Declaration of Independence, declaring an autonomous and free Negro state.

Unfortunately, during those few years, France had undergone yet another revolution. The response of the new French emperor – Napoleon Bonaparte – was to send a massive force of soldiers and warships to reclaim the island. However, Haiti's revolution was not over yet.

Those Mulatto leaders were persuasive. Napoleon had discovered several exiled Mulatto warriors that Louverture had defeated and sent away years earlier and brought them back to the island to fight alongside his French troops. Several of Louverture's generals had defected to the French side of the fight. They believed life would be better for the enslaved people under French rule – not knowing that Napoleon had secretly sent his army with orders to restore the slavery system after they crushed the uprising.

In late 1802, Napoleon's men promised Louverture and the island's freedom if he gave his army over to the French and surrendered control of the island. When he complied, convinced that his generals might be correct, they kidnapped him, shipped him to France, locked him in a dungeon, and quietly reinstated slavery in Haiti.

They had, however, misjudged Louverture's generals. As it became evident that the French intended to re-enslave Haiti, those generals sneaked into the countryside and re-ignited the insurrection. As the combat erupted across the island, the French forces found themselves in an untenable situation. As yellow fever infected their troops, the British imposed a naval blockade on Haiti's major ports. Napoleon shifted his focus away from the islands and toward his land campaigns in Europe.

The Haitians fought the final battle of the revolution in November 1803. On January 1, 1804, the country's leader, Jean-Jacques Dessalines, re-instituted Louverture's Constitution and declared himself ruler-for-life of the new, independent Haiti,' after the island's historical name.

The occurrence astounded Napoleon and the rest of the world. United States President Thomas Jefferson was so outraged by the revolt that he asked that his country impose an economic embargo on Haiti; because the American South was slave-dependent, the United States Congress agreed. US ships were permitted to enter Haiti, but Haitian boats were not allowed to enter US ports, preventing Haiti from benefiting from the economic superpower. The restriction went into place in 1806 and would continue for nearly two centuries until lifted.

Consider the local community and Haitian national leaders at the time. The responsibility of being in control was hard enough; add to that the challenge of ruling a group of people who had not experienced peace in a long time, and you had a constantly turbulent situation. Where would you begin?

Except for those who were fortunate enough to have been exposed to it, education was essentially non-existent. Of course, there were several chores to perform, but you can't pay people, and you certainly can't force them to work for free – not without fostering the same slave mindset people had just murdered to remove.

You may have thousands of ideas, but most usually come from experience, imitation, and collaboration. The leaders had none of those, considering the path they had just traveled down. However, they did come up with Corvée, which means "you pay taxes in labor instead of money." That way, they could get people who had no money to do the work the government needed to complete, and the government did not need to have money to get the job done.

(I remember a version other than what I found described in my research. One of the most memorable moments I remember growing up in Haiti was spending my summer vacation on my grandfather's farm. I was ten years old; I remember being awakened by a group of people, primarily men, chanting outside. The laughter and their coffee cups' clicking sound projected an air of family and a unique type of bonded friendship. The gathering happened every morning at different houses during the planting and harvesting seasons. The purpose was to help each other plant and harvest crops without hiring workers. They called that community effort 'Corvée.')

The most precious source of income for any community to grow is its ability to produce something. Haiti had plenty of tobacco, sugar cane, indigo, and other agricultural items that the world could use. Unfortunately, the less Haiti exported as the revolution wore on, the weaker it got. The weakness scenario became a recurring theme. Over the next two hundred years, many governments formed, and the many disasters that struck forced Haitian farmers to abandon their farms or destroy their crops.

For example, when Papa-Doc Duvalier brought truckloads of farmers to Port-au-Prince to join the Ton-Ton Macoute, he crippled Haiti's economic ability because so many farmers decided to stay in the city, and many farms were left empty.

Finding the bona fide answer to why Haiti is the most impoverished nation is hugely controversial. On the political front, the government could not do the type of analysis to reveal the real culprit without touching the nerves of those with preconceived notions in their heart. Hence, there is room to stick a blame label on everyone involved.

Haitian history shows most enslavers were men with evil intentions so deep in their hearts that they cultivated little regard for other human beings. Many economic opportunities declined because they came from white people or Mullatos and were thus unsafe. As a result, the human beings who were the victims of their heinous acts developed a long-lasting hatred that contributed to the Haitian economy's demise.

But for all of that, the Haitian people are proud. The Haitian people are proud of their unique culinary traditions. The Haitian people are proud of their music and culture.

If I could inventory factors that have had the most devastating effects or worsened Haiti's people's misery during the last few years, the United States would be at the top. I mentioned the two-hundred-year trade embargo, but that is the initial act. On June 25th, 1994, the U.S. government strengthened the blockade, prohibiting trade between the U.S. and Haiti and any ships from one country visiting the other. By no coincidence, the Haitian government's debt doubled between 1995 and 2010.

The United States consistently examined Haiti's politics, and whenever something happens that the U.S. disapproves of, the economic backlash is instant and painful. For example, in the 2000 elections in Haiti, the candidates favored by Washington D.C. lost. In response, the U.S. government called for the Inter-American Development Bank and the European Union to stop offering development loans to Haiti's government and enterprises.

I live in America, and there have been times when I was listening to educated lawmakers reason with self-satisfaction as they participate in economically crippling a group of people already in distress, and my heart bleeds genuinely. Their reasons usually revolve around the goal of putting pressure on an evil government or lousy practice with the hope of helping the masses. Unfortunately, it never works as intended. The opposite usually happens. When the targeted government officials are finally ousted, they would have stolen substantial money before leaving. Most of the time, these officials would live abroad in luxury while the population continued to suffer.

When the American States Organization met on June 25th in, 1994, with the specific goal of making the embargo against Haiti efficient, how many poor people from Haiti had any representation? How many people in that group understood the real impact the restriction would have on Haiti's people? One can argue that the people of the ousted government of Jean-Bertrand Aristide needed to learn a valuable lesson.

Chapter 26

Borlette or Gambling of a Culture

Before the 2010 earthquake, many houses had a small bureau used as a lottery business. After the quake had annihilated numerous neighborhoods in Haiti, even people on the mountainside had transferred from one hillside to a different locality to continue with the operation. They erected camps along the roadside with bedsheets, branches, tarps, corrugated tin, and plywood. The lotto system, commonly known as Borlette, thrived in chaos. Thus, one continues to survive, notwithstanding building states and impairments.

Amid all the debris, people set up little tables or kiosks the size of a telephone booth with Borlette signs painted in various colors. Then, they went to work selling numbers for the next lottery drawing.

Since very few buildings were not affected by Port-Au-Prince's capital, hundreds of thousands had to flee to the countryside. The quake has decimated the city's population, and countless little businesses, including the Borlette gig, had to escape.

The Borlette phenomenon formed a population of dreamers. It cost very little to partake in the game, requiring one Haitian gourde to purchase a lottery number. In 2017, that was the equivalent of $ 0.016 U. S dollars.

The earthquake has touched over half of the population, yet you can find thousands of locations to buy Borlette tickets. Driving around, you can see Borlette locations in front of 70% of the houses. The construction of these buildings was very modest and even endured the violent shaking of the quake.

Nowadays, it is much easier to locate a Borlette location than a school.

The Haitian people take the Borlette game very seriously. For them, it is one way to survive the unthinkable suite of sufferings life has bestowed upon them. The Borlette had offered them a mode to hope for food, water, and even medicine. As a result, most of the population plays the game.

Dreaming was essential to surviving the game's oddness and difficulty. I mean actual dreams. We had books that interpreted people's dreams, and they purchased numbers based on the type of vision they had the previous night.

When I was growing up, I remember when we went to church on Sundays, we would walk down to the church, and the church would be in service, and you would see a lot of young men outside with their radios on, and you would hear broadcasting of the lottery in Spanish. At first, the lottery would come out on Saturdays, but when the government of Cuba turned Communist, people did not want to have the Borlette over any more Sunday mornings at 10 o'clock when the church was going on. Therefore, people used it as a lottery; the Borlette was a raffle.

The way you played was to take a piece of paper. They had three prizes: The first one was $50, the second award was $15, and the third prize was $10. They never go over 100 numbers; from one to 100, they sell one to each person. If the lottery vendor sells all the numbers, he can make $25. So, most people who play lose $1, and those who win could collect $50, $15, or $10. At the basic level, it was the perfect game for everyone.

Borlette got out of hand at home because people wanted to know who won. As I said, Borlette was broadcast every Sunday morning at ten o'clock in Spanish. The Spanish lottery usually is five or six numbers, but they only care about the last two.

Borlette players believed they had a connection with the spirit world during their night vision, and faith dictated how they should play following moving images revealed to them the night before.

In the whole country, people get up in the morning; the first thing they do before breakfast is get together and ask each other what dreams they had the night before.

I remember my parents would get us up in the morning and ask us what kind of vision we had; every kid, even those who could hardly talk, was not immune to this type of interrogation. A lucky child talks about a dream and the number of related wins.

How do they equate nightly visions with numbers? You may ask. They had a dream dictionary; the numerology book was like a dictionary. A number corresponds to every object for every dream you have. But, of course, some things had more than two corresponding numbers.

If your father appeared in your dream, it could mean the number 7 would be a good number to play. If you saw a cocoa tree, they construed it as number 10. They had a name for every situation. Everybody was making numerology books about dreams, and sometimes it worked, and sometimes it did not work, but we found people were relying too much on those revelations. They risked every single penny they had, then pawned their belongings. The obsession with Borlette has caused families to split sometimes. Obsessive wives or husbands would gamble with borrowed money and later could not repay their debts.

The Borlette became an epidemic; it became a part-time job for the people in Haiti because everybody was doing it, from grade school to high school students, university students, and parents. Even small children were selling numbers for 10 cents or two cents, they were selling numbers, and they had a prize for first, second, and third place. It was free, and the government never had anything to say about this because everybody was making money from it, but many people lost everything they had.

The second way they went about dreams was an invocation of the spirits. To invoke the spirits, people went to see a Houngan, the voodoo priest, Mambo, or whoever they wanted, and they would ask them for numbers or go to the cemetery if the mother and father were dead. They would ask the mother or father about the spirits. So, they had a different way of invoking the spirits, they would call Satan's presence, and if they went like this, many times, people would give their mother's and father's souls away to find out what number was going to win the next day.

The other bad thing about Borlette was that if someone didn't have the money to pay for a number, they would pawn their furniture, clothes, and even their cars to raise funds for a lottery number. The numbers are different prices; they can be any price the person selling them wants them to be. If it is $1,000 for a lotto number, you can imagine how much money a person could win. If you bought a lotto number for $1,000, you had a chance to win the first prize, which was $50,000, so the winners made a lot of money from the Borlette, but people used to lose a lot of money.

I witnessed a portion of one incident where a man visited a voodoo priest to ask how to invoke the spirits, so the priest gave him instructions on how to summon the spirits and send them back. He was supposed to leave his house and go to a specific place by midnight. He was living in the countryside and had to travel on horseback. So, he took his horse, a couple of friends, and all the ingredients he needed to summon the spirit. He went to the appointed place. When he got there, he invoked the deity, but unfortunately, he panicked and did not remember how to send it back.

Some people call this the "calling of the stars." They believe that someone calls the stars down to give them a number, but they call the devil's spirit to come down and provide them with a lotto number. When the worshipped deity appears, the man loses his nerve, and if you panic, the god might punish him. The following day they found the horse dead, part of the horse was skinned alive, and on the horse's bones, there was the number 70 written. They found the man also dead; he had been trying to run about 500 feet away from the horse. The following Sunday, number 70 was the number that won the first prize. Many people believe that they can talk to the dead. So, they have a ceremony that they do.

The Borlette epidemic became widely known and is still commonly known in Haiti. People go to great lengths to find out about the numbers; some Catholic people say they worship the rainbow; they have a special place called Sodo where they worship. In this situation, the water comes down from the mountains, and thousands of people pray to find out about the numbers.

Chapter 27

Road to America

Medical School Ambition

The agony of preparing for a final during my high school years was still apparent in my mind. Even though it had been over two years, I had failed to find dependable employment.

I was secretly enjoying the noble purpose of pursuing a medical profession. To my knowledge, French was the official language, especially in teaching in Haiti's medical schools.

Day after day, the ambition tormented me. I consulted with friends to learn more about the practice. I proceeded that way to prevent traps and to comprehend the loopholes. Obtaining professional knowledge in biology, chemistry, physics, and physiology was among the obstacles to passing medical examinations. Furthermore, vagueness in admission requirements caused even the most bright, most ambitious students to fail without knowing why.

I struggled to come up with the money and grudgingly paid for entrance after a buddy advised me to spend a couple hundred dollars attending pre-med programs. Teachers gave classes during the summer and arranged exams for September.

I did not learn about the creation of Burnett International University School of Medicine until 2002. Burnett provided English language training for physicians and nurses! Other private institutions, such as Quisqueya and King Henry Christophe, as well as the governmental State University of Haiti, appeared in the region.

The drive to school was excruciatingly hot, and the country was in the grip of one of the most terrible droughts in recent memory. Copley news services' Edwards Neyland stated:

"More than 300,000 people in the northwest, mostly small farmers, and their families, had seen very little rain. One could look at the parches and cracks on the ground's surface. The heat practically destroyed the corn, sorghum, and bean crops, and only cactus and a few anemic-appearing trees dot the scorched hills.

After a survey in late May of that year, American Ambassador to Haiti Heyward Isham said the disaster called for U.S. emergency assistance. He authorized U.S. Food for Peace foods already in the country and requested disaster relief funds. By early summer, the food had reached more than 146,000 people."

Students have few options for getting to school. You could walk in the sun through trash-filled, dust-swirled streets or take the bus. Second, it was usual to hail a local cab, and no more than one or two persons might ride together. The other option was to endure the agony of being a passenger in a camionette, transporting up to 20 people at a time.

These camionette drivers were unlicensed, unregulated, brightly painted 'taxi vehicles,' offering little more than a harsh metal or wooden bench surface to sit on and bouncing down the road hard enough to rattle your teeth.

The pre-med program attendees came from a variety of backgrounds. Some were from well-known and visibly wealthy families. Others came from abroad, and a handful from aspirant middle-class parents who desired more for their children. My parents were completely unaware of the procedure.

All I could do was convey my desire, and they wished me well. Due to the drought, I would spend the entire day at school with only the breakfast I had had from my mother in my stomach and would not even consider obtaining anything else until I returned home.

On the first day of school, I expected a formal setting, possibly a building with more than one room and multiple medical professors teaching different courses. Instead, I entered a long tent in a yard with over 200 students and three lecturers in front of me, all fighting to hear one other. We were all acclimated to the living circumstances of the time and did not lament the situation since we knew better.

There was a lovely French lady dressed in a white coat. We could see her name and title on her left chest. She did, however, appear quite pale to me. The girl on my left mumbled that she was from Paris, while the student to my right insisted that she was from Quebec. "All I want to know is if she's an excellent instructor." "Does it make a difference?" I contributed to the low-key discourse.

She had her long silky hair in a bow behind her neck. When she moved oppositely, the tip of her improperly braided ponytail swung left and right.

As she took the microphone to begin the typical roll call, the other two teachers frantically rushed about the room, ensuring each student had a good seat for the day.

On the left, the older doctor distributed us handouts, while the one on the right walked row by row to verify everyone registered correctly (that is, had they paid the required cost). After a few phone calls, I heard my name and said, "Here," to which someone handed me the curriculum. I examined the brochure and saw that sixty percent of the course was physiology and anatomy of the human body – and then I realized I didn't have the book they were using. The cost of the book exceeded the cost of the class.

On the first day, I felt entirely out of place. Students answered questions correctly and incorrectly while professors intensely posed them. I was on the New York Stock Exchange floor as I patiently followed their patterns.

I looked for a study partner for two days. Finally, one of the instructors saw our problems and encouraged students to start sharing and copying the books.

Every day following that, when I came, pupils gathered in groups and quizzed one another. Some of us picked it quickly, and it was essential to arrive earlier than average to study and recall body parts and try our best to predict the following round of questions. Everyone considered their book to be as holy as their own life.

I spent the entire three summer months taking lessons there. However, when the time arrived for the exam in September, I immediately realized I was not ready. I later discovered that I lacked the necessary political contacts to be approved and qualified to take the test.

My lack of exposure to pre-med didn't aid my interest in other fields of study.

I didn't know who to contact. So I wandered about for years, thinking about the subjects that may have been on the test. I kept telling myself. Could it have been similar to the MCAT? "What is my next step?"

Chapter 28

First trip to the United States

My travel to the United States was yet another divine intervention. It is usual for parents to try to send their children to the United States to study, and they prefer that they pursue careers in engineering or medicine. My father wanted me to be a doctor because he believed I was clever enough, and I wanted to attain that objective.

I took the exam but did not pass due to government issues. I still wanted to come to America and live a different life. I never participated in any Voodoo rituals. I appreciated the freedom to worship God however I pleased and the opportunity to live a better life.

To reach my goal, I started to learn English every day.

I taught myself English in high school by studying one to five words daily. At night, I'd find a quiet area on top of a cement roof and tune my shortwave radio to catch the "Voice of America" broadcasting over the airways.

I would occasionally listen to John Vernon McGee's show. According to Wikipedia, Pastor McGee began broadcasting on the Bible Radio Network in 1967. Before retiring in January 1970, he would complete each Bible book. Those two and a half years weren't enough.

He finished another Bible study in five years. Every every day, he is translated into over 100 languages and aired.

My English grade caught the attention of my high school principal. I had no notion Pastor McGee's accent was unusual until I moved to the United States. I gradually began to grasp what he was saying.

He used to operate a car rental business. His visitors were mainly from the United States. Every time a visitor arrived at the school, I was one of the pupils he would show off to the foreigners. This engagement with folks who could speak the language gave me a firm foundation.

I decided to create an English club in my Seventh-day Adventist church. A group of friends and I would travel to the Seventh-day Adventist Seminary, and missionary students from the United States would come and stay there. The school administrator noticed my English was a lot better than most Haitian teachers, and he offered me a position as an English teacher. I taught English for three years while trying to enter medical school in Port-au-Prince. I attended pre-med school in Delmas during the day and taught English at night.

My teaching job was in Carrefour. Carrefour is where many cars and commercial trucks must go through to reach Leogane, Jacmel, and other small towns due to its location. In 2003, the official census estimated a population of 373,916 for Carrefour, which almost doubled in 2015 to 511,345. That is more than half a million people in a small area. The Seminary location was in the middle of Carrefour in Diquini, and the SDA church operated one of the most advanced hospitals there.

During my time there, the hospital was not as developed as today. In 2016, SDA opened a state-of-the-art surgical suite, a private multi-med clinic, and a new laboratory. The church hosted Christian missionaries from different parts of the United States and other parts of the world. Weekly, I attended Sabbath services to improve my English. There, I met one of these young missionaries. She came from Union College in Lincoln, Nebraska. Her name was Terri Melancon.

She was born in Huntsville, Alabama, and attended Nebraska school. Her father, James Melancon, was an Oakwood University Professor I admired after meeting him. My relationship with Terri was rather peculiar and hard to describe. It was merely a unique opportunity to become fluent in the English language and learn as much as I could about the American people's culture. To her, I was nothing more than someone she needed to groom in the art of sophistication. We spent a lot of time together. I was driving a big yellow Jeep Wagoneer. I still cannot recall the year since my dad had altered it several times with parts and engines from different models. She needed me, and I needed her. I drove her around the capital of Port-au-Prince and the surrounding communities and frequented restaurants and other places I would have never visited if it weren't for her. As our friendship grew, we became a never-publicly announced "boyfriend and girlfriend."

For a long time, I lived with the understanding that the relationship was strictly platonic. One day, I shared with Terri that I was applying for a visa to migrate to Canada. Her reaction was astounding. Terri responded with anger implying why I would go to Canada without exploring my options with her first. I explained to her that I was profoundly perplexed and thought I did not have anything to prevent pursuing my dream. She asked me to wait while exploring other avenues without additional details.

The following day Sunday, I picked her up and drove to Petion-Ville. It is a town located not far from Port-au-Prince in one of the suburbs. The commune is in the east hills. The city took the name of Alexandre Sabes Petion, one of the country's four founding fathers. While on the road, she said: "I have great news." I said: "What news?". I was not expecting anything special other than getting our rapport to the next level. "I talked to the Dean at Union College, and I believe there is a way you can attend school in Lincoln, Nebraska, and hopefully, you and I can get to know each other better," she added. I was speechless for a short period. To her, it felt like an eternity. I ended the silence by saying: "That would be great, except for the money."

She said, "God has opened a door for you; just trust he will provide the means for you to succeed." We spent an unbelievable amount of time on the phone with the Union College Administrative office the following days. Before discussing anything with my parents, I waited until we had all the details. Two weeks had passed; I had not heard anything yet from the States.

Meanwhile, I made sure I had a passport and went to the Consulate, and when I got there, the Consulate looked at my papers, and she looked at me, and she was very interested in me; she said I could speak English very well. She said, "Well, we could help you, but you don't have enough money to pay for the four years you want to go to Union College to learn Business Administration."

She turned me down. I had to tell my father they had turned down my request, but I did not give up hope because I knew the Lord had a plan for my life. I knew the Lord had an idea for everything that happened to me in my whole life, so I did not give up. I prayed to the Lord and prayed and prayed every day. Sometimes I felt frustrated; sometimes, I got discouraged. The entire world looked black because I thought nothing else was exciting anymore.

The American Embassy has always been one of the fascinating places to visit because a "yes and no" answer after asking for a visa can change someone's life forever.

After graduating from high school and failing miserably at getting admission to medical school, I was hopelessly floating around with a teaching position at the Seventh-day Adventist seminary, which happened to be located precisely at the epicenter of the recent earthquake.

It was a unique position with no guarantee of securing a promising future. Like others were doing at the time, I spent months getting my passport and all the necessary papers ready. I made several trips to secure an appointment to see the consulate for a visa. I remember when the day came, I had a letter of approval from Union College in Lincoln, Nebraska, a valid permit, and another note securing my room at the dormitory at UC.

I approached the consulate with near-perfect English (for someone who had not left Haiti even once). She complimented me for what I achieved and said, "I will have my stamps ready to apply to your passport – if you can come back within a week with a check for six thousand dollars. This check will make me feel better, knowing that you will be able to pay at least for your first year of school in Nebraska."

To me, that was the kiss of death. Most people in Haiti probably never make six thousand dollars in their entire lifetime, let alone come up with that kind of money within a week. I went home that day destroyed. Yet, despite my devastation, I had enough courage to stop at my dad's shop. From what I can only think of as a genuine miracle, I arrived while my dad had a relevant conversation with one of his patrons. The gentleman bragged about spending ten thousand dollars in college and dormitory funds for his son in New Jersey.

I pulled my dad aside and explained to him what had happened. "It's amazing," my father told his patron, "We were talking about your son, and now I have the same situation, but unfortunately, I will never be able to afford that kind of money."

"Nonsense!" His patron said. "They don't want the money – they want to see the check. Why don't I lend you the money? Then, I can go to the bank and bring you a check tomorrow. Then, Robert can proudly return to the consulate next week, show her the check, and you can return the money to me."

"Can you do that?" my dad said with a fantastic look.

To my surprise, that blessed man showed up two days later with the check. When I arrived at the consulate a week later, she was stunned and silent. She did not say a word – she just looked at me, blinked a few times, and mechanically stamped my passport. That was my last (and best) experience

Chapter 29

How Faith in God grew

I did my best to keep my father from contacting voodoo priests to address my concerns while creating a viable plan to travel to the United States. As I know my father, whenever a situation emerged, his traditional approach was to take steps in the only direction he knew how. He thought contacting a medium would offer him the best outcome regardless of the circumstances.

I'd say no when that happens because I was confident God would provide for me. Please do not go to anybody about me, I would beg him. I'll be OK; the Lord will see that everything works out for the best. I would kindly ask him to let me make my own decisions because I greatly respected him. He usually acknowledged my choices are important to me. When this approach succeeded, I complimented him for keeping his promise of giving me the independence I desperately needed to grow up.

We considered getting a loan on the property numerous times as the desire to help me became tenfold. We understood it was a risky gambling venture because he worked too hard and patiently to build the house. The idea of putting the whole family in financial jeopardy was not practical. Should we have taken that route, we'd have had to collaborate with some of his more financially secure or dangerous buddies. No existing banks in the area were sophisticated enough to handle this transaction. We reasoned the situation from every viewpoint but came to no satisfying conclusions. As a result, we abandoned the plan.

We stayed focused and worked together to find solutions to our condition. Even today, I'm unaware whether my father consulted a medium about this situation. On my side, I continued to pray: Lord, you are my God, and I love you; I know you will make things work for me, and I want to believe in You. I want to express how much I adore my mum and father. They have been quite helpful to me.

My blood pressure typically decreases when I let down my guard to pray like this. I generally achieve perfect serenity and rapidly become stronger to move forward with fixing my concerns.

When I reflect on that circumstance, with a huge family on my own, there are a few things I wish I had known when I was younger.

I prayed most hours of the day and night for God's guidance on what I should do with my life. As Terri's conversations with the college administration started to bear fruit, she spoke with one of the professors about the issue. Reports began circulating that I was ready to quit due to my inspiration to continue my studies abroad. The seminary students were nearing the end of their final examinations. Terry would return to Nebraska, and I had no certainty that the seminary would extend my teaching contract for the following year.

That's when I realized things were heading in the right direction. God could have already answered my prayers.

Finally, the formal application letter arrived. One of the conditions in the letter was guidelines for TOEFL. The Test of English as a Foreign Language is a standardized test used to assess the English language proficiency of non-native speakers seeking admission to English-speaking colleges. It was a requirement for my admittance to Union College. To cover the TOEFL's first school passes,

I required at least $6000.00. I was unconcerned about the exam because I was already teaching basic English at the Seventh-day Adventist seminary.

My only and most significant predicament was simple: I had no way of explaining to my father that I had discovered a means to travel to the United States, but I needed that type of money to make it happen. On the other hand, six thousand dollars was a lot of money, especially for someone in Haiti. Terri and I talked about it, and she told Union College about it. That amount was simple compared to today's requirements.

According to the Union College Academics website informational page, tuition and fees for undergraduate studies in 2022-2023 cost around $34,920 for the year, which includes general fees, room rent with a roommate, and campus food.

That made me feel even more uneasy. I quickly learned that I did not have to pay the registration fee. However, the American embassy will want me to prove that I had the money in the bank to obtain a student visa. The Consulate also required proof that my parents could handle the bill that would come in the future. It meant the same to me either way because I had no clue from whom or where I would acquire the money.

I was gloomy and anxious for several weeks. I'd battle with having a certain amount of faith that might keep me from becoming depressed. The struggle was brutal and exhausting.

One day, my father explained the problem to one of his clients. This customer successfully sent two children to the United States under identical circumstances.

"Boss Ornil," as everyone called my dad, said the clients, "we have numerous projects coming up; we can deposit the needed money in a bank account under your son's name." After he gets his visa, you may utilize part of the money for your current project.

We were all surprised and relieved that God had responded to our prayers. To secure the visa, we did just that. Once in the United States, I worked various jobs while attending school. It took a few years to pay off my college loans, but God provided a means for me to accomplish it.

I have struggled, and the Lord has been with me. My message to anyone who reads this book is that anything is possible if you trust the Lord, no matter your circumstances.

Both my parents are now gone. I hope that they have made peace with God. So they can be there with him when Jesus returns, as promised in the Bible. When they got involved with voodoo, one of us kids was sick, and they pledged themselves. So, I pray that the Lord will be with them and save their souls.

Chapter 30

My Father's Illness

My father suffered two significant strokes five years before his death. After the strokes, he was bedridden for three years at his house in Port-au-Prince; my sister Natasha, mother, and brother Benjamin cared for him. Before visiting Nebraska and spending some time in New York, he had the lucky chance to visit the United States twice. I thought about him much, but maybe not as much as I should have because I was his eldest son.

The following account began on a snowy day in Nebraska on January 4, 2001. That week appeared to have a million things that needed my attention.

I'd been attempting to keep an appointment with my dentist for three weeks, whom I hadn't seen in over two years. I had begun to feel ill in my mouth, and when I tried to consume hot food, I would endure excruciating discomfort.

I couldn't afford a dentist's treatment since I started working for First Data Resources, an Omaha-based credit card processing firm. I worked there as a software developer, and after two years, they began to lay employees off. I've been with this organization for about five years and have been a part of some of the most beneficial software deployments built by the methodology and tools department.

Unfortunately, management informed us that they had to lay off around 400 brilliant computer programmers and managers in March 2000, followed by another 600 for the year.

Because I've worked in information technology for a long time, I discovered this via my experiences. Companies who hire me as a consultant rather than just a developer may gain the most from my knowledge.

In March of that year, I started working as an analyst and supervisor for a new software business. After a few projects, I concluded my personality did not fit well with their current methodology and characters. As a result, I submitted my resume to a different company.

That new organization quickly accepted me, and I began working as a senior consultant at Norstan Consulting in August.

As stated in a publication about Norstan in 1993, it became evident that offering services rather than just selling equipment offered greater financial rewards. As a result, Norstan shifted from a company focused on selling products to one that specializes in integrating communications and information technology systems. It later purchased North Carolina-based Prima and Minnesota-based Connect Computer Inc., two technology consulting companies. To become Norstan Consulting, the two companies have combined their effort working with the business's current professional services division. With these acquisitions, Norstan expanded its phone and video operations to provide premium data communications services.

I worked on various projects, including substance misuse tracking and document imaging systems.

After many successful software installations with this new consulting firm, I was fortunate to earn the respect of everyone, even the president.

Suzy Wilkins comes to mind. She was my immediate financial manager, and we had a great working relationship. She was an astute lady.

Working as a consultant was one of the most rewarding jobs I'd ever done. The thought of not having a direct supervisor appealed to me. My true boss was the client. I might be as delighted as ever if I achieved satisfactory outcomes. My finance supervisor recognized my accomplishments and offered me a bonus regularly. She once paid for my wife's three-day working vacation so she could accompany me to one of my remote location projects.

As a consultant, I assessed work in Omaha's headquarters and chose whether to meet with clients for final approval of work. I used to travel to other states once a week and then return home on weekends.

One week, I had to submit a work plan that required the permission of a third-party vendor to acquire a new product. The expense of designing software from scratch was too expensive. There was a retired physician by the name of Dr. Goldberg. He owned companies in Florida, Wisconsin, and Minneapolis. He was straightforward to work with and one of the most successful businesspeople I have ever encountered.

He resided in Miami but also owned a home in the Milwaukee region. I appreciated him for his achievements. Dr. Goldberg has the same personality traits as my father. He was the type of person who knew what he wanted and when he wanted it. He built a respected and slightly intimidating environment around him, particularly for those who did not know him well. We knew that Dr. Goldberg's business would need four to six weeks after we submitted the proposal before they could offer us a concrete strategy for completing the project, but we figured those weeks would fly by.

My basement flooded following a major downpour six months before I started working in Milwaukee. The sump pump had broken down. When I phoned the insurance company, they agreed to pay for the removal of our basement walls and carpet replacement. I wanted to save money, so I renovated the basement myself instead of hiring a contractor. The cellar was still unfinished due to the upheaval of shifting employment. That was a chance for me to spend time with my girls together as a family.

One of the apartment complexes I owned in Lincoln, Nebraska, roughly sixty miles from where I resided in Elkhorn, started to give me nothing except legal issues with the installation.

Thus, I felt something hollering for my attention, which is why I didn't overthink about my father. He had been ailing for some time, and my mind had become accustomed to the thought that he might die sometime, but not soon— not now. So I went to the dentist that day, unaware that my father was unwell.

Sitting on the dentist's chair, I was captivated by all the new technologies that had emerged since my last visit.

On a twenty-one-inch screen, I could see the inside of my lips all the way o my throat. A camera mounted at the end of the dental instrument made my mind go wild with crazy thoughts. I began to consider all technological possibilities as he probed inside my mouth. The pen's size apparatus had a light in addition to the camera so he could inspect it thoroughly.

Talking with one's mouth full on a dentist's chair has always been the butt of many jokes. I sat on the dental chair in astonishment as he moved the little device, showing me my neglected gums and all the work he'd have to perform. As my mouth filled with cotton on the side, he asked me questions to which I couldn't give him a discernable answer.

All I could think about was how much this agony would cost me," I thought. I immediately resolved to floss and brush at more regular intervals. The surgery would restore my mouth's natural function and erase my constant foul breath. When I left the dentist's office, it was freezing outdoors. The country was enduring one of the harshest winters in nearly a century.

Chapter 31

Phone Calls

The phone rang as soon as I got back to my office. My sister from New York was speaking on the other end. I hardly understood a word of what she was saying. All I could hear was something about dad, or as we called him, "Papa," in Creole, "my dad." At that point, I realized my father had passed away.

I had never felt like that before; something different was taking place. I experienced both vulnerability and wellness. I had the impression that my father was telling me to "be strong and in control" in his native tongue. However, I was at a loss for words to comfort my sister. Nothing I could say to her to comfort her while sobbing would have been helpful.

My sister's call ended, and I then got another call. Even worse, this call was disturbing. It was my brother Gabriel, the youngest child in the family. What's going on with our dad, Gabriel may ask? I stressed that he needed to stay well because our father had passed away. I still thought of Gabriel as the family's infant, even though he was married and had children. Gabriel had been about six or seven when I had initially left Haiti. I had sobbed when I left him behind and thought about him for months.

The reality was beginning to sink in.

My wife then called, so I answered and briefed her on the circumstances.

I had to choose now. I thought I was ready for whatever came next and knew I had to be in Haiti as quickly as possible to be with my family for the burial.

"How can I proceed financially from here?" I continued to think. Both the flight to Haiti and the funeral costs would be expensive. I had been planning to sell a few equities to cover outstanding expenses for months. I still had some shares in my retirement account from the business that had fired me. Whenever I considered selling them, I had a voice telling me to hold off unless a problematic situation occurred. I thus made the first move by contacting my Norstan financial supervisor.

I stated what had happened and that I needed some assistance. The financial supervisor's name was Suzy Wilkins. She immediately phoned the accounting division and gave them the case details. They rejected her request that she assisted me and made it plain that they had no power to aid since they weren't a loan organization. I was grateful she had even attempted when she phoned me back and explained the circumstance. I didn't have any higher hopes than her. I was shocked, though, when she called and said, "Guess what?"

She urged that the accounting division help me after communicating with the business president. Added, "We will do everything we can to make this happen. You have contributed significantly to this business."

I told myself to praise God. She said to mention the required amount, and we will advance it to you. I informed her that although I had some savings, they might be able to loan me $2,000 if it wasn't enough; I would let her know later. She said no problem. The next day, she deposited the promised amount into my account.

I accessed my Charles Schwab account through the internet instead of calling and sold 100 shares of the stocks in my retirement account. When I phoned my broker later to ask when I might get the cash, he informed me that, per company policy, I would not get any money for three working days. We'll see about that, I responded.

I went to the Charles Schwab location, sat with the broker's manager, and described my circumstance. No issue, he responded. In three business days, we can offer you the cash and more cash if you require it. That ought to get me started, I told him.

My wife seldom participates in business or financial decisions, but she handled things like a pro on that particular day. She was on the phone as the most outstanding professional secretary in the world. Within twenty-four hours, I was ready to fly to Port-au-Prince, Haiti, after she used the Internet to book my tickets.

At 3:10 that Thursday, January 4, 2001, my father passed away. My family took me to the airport on the Friday after that. When I flew across the nation for work, my wife or the entire family would almost always join me at the airport, but this time was different.

My friends and acquaintances called and emailed me to express their condolences. However, there was one call that I will never forget coming from my wife's sister, Kathy Ryan. When I got it, I was still at the airport, ready to get on the plane.

That day, Kathy called and expressed a special kind of affection. Although she didn't say much, the tone of her voice lingered in my head for days. I always got the impression that Kathy only accepted me, the kids, and my wife because of her demeanor sometimes —I knew from her manners that my other sister-in-law, Jo, adored the kids and me. Though I knew I was incorrect, the thought nonetheless crossed my mind. I recognized my sister's concern for me for the first time since my wife, and I were married, and I cherish that.

Given that I was going through a terrible moment, all of these sentiments were pure conjecture. People's actions can occasionally be misleading. I have seen individuals who, on the outside, seem obnoxious yet, within, have enormous hearts. Whether genuinely extroverts or introverts, society does not fairly treat these people. Don't judge a book by its cover, as they say.

The final person to kiss me farewell was my wife. I reflected that I was on a mission and could not afford to lose it throughout the journey and that my father would not approve of anything different.

Chapter 32

In Dallas/Fort Worth

On schedule, the aircraft touched down at the Dallas/Fort Worth airport. It seemed like 10 hours had passed, although I was only out for ten minutes. Walking from one gate to the next appeared to take a while. You must pay attention, Bob, or you may miss your connection; I kept stressing.

According to the airport kiosks, the airline set my flight departure from Gate A27 for our subsequent connection in Miami. I awaited the train to take me to the following terminal. I descended the stairs and started walking toward the station because I wanted to use the concourse. Even though I just had to wait five minutes, it seemed like hours. There were countless people at the airport, yet I still felt alone in a weird, ruthless world. I turned to my left and saw a sign pointing the newly arrived passengers in the right direction.

There were more than 100 individuals on the train as I boarded it with the other passengers. Others sat with their bags on their laps, while some stood and gripped the safety rails. Are we all going to the gate? I questioned the individuals sitting next to me. Thank God everyone agreed. So I was heading in the correct direction.

A young woman from West Africa was selling technical accessories for cell phones when I arrived at Gate A27. One of the devices caught my interest. The shopkeeper informed me several times that electricity was hard to get in Haiti.

They were using AC Anywhere adapters, and when the power went out, I believed I could take this adaptor from a car to charge my computer.

It could be beneficial for my brother Benjamin as well. I asked the lovely African girl about the cost of the adaptor. She said, "Ninety-nine dollars," in a gentle, slightly quiet voice. I took the adaptor even though I knew it should only cost $59 and handed her $100, instructing her to keep the difference. I boarded the aircraft after the flight attendants' last call.

Chapter 33

On My Way to Miami

I unenthusiastically looked for my assigned seat number, sat down, and buckled my seat belt. I was holding my cell phone and mulling over my next move. I checked to ensure my phone was still working when I realized I needed to change my system from the A to the B antenna to send and receive calls anywhere. So, I did that, and then I called my brother Estephan in Miami to tell him of my arrival. I told him I was on the airplane waiting for liftoff and that I would call him as soon as we landed in Miami.

I felt somewhat anesthetized throughout the flight all over my body; maybe it was my imagination. I kept thinking, "I must keep my mind occupied with other thoughts, or I will go crazy." Finally, I grabbed my computer and began working on my website.

Haiti is always in mayhem, which has worsened since I left twenty-three years ago. Before I had left Nebraska, I had asked my wife to transfer money to me once I arrived in Haiti since I had no idea how much the funeral would cost. Things have changed dramatically and, unfortunately, not for the better.

I arrived in Miami around 11:30 that night. I called my brother and asked him to come and pick me up at the airport.

I went to the baggage claim area and looked for the suitcase my wife had packed the night before. I had no idea what she had put in it, but she often packs my bag when I travel, and I knew it would have whatever I needed. No matter how frequently she and I encountered difficulties, she always reminded me how extremely efficient she could be. This wonderful wife of mine has unique qualities, and it is hard to find them anywhere else in this universe.

Within a few minutes after locating my suitcase, I received a phone call from my brother Stephan. He told me to wait for him outside the airport's main entrance.

I stepped outside and found a crowded street Taxicabs and private vehicles everywhere, jammed one against the other, and shuttle buses from motels, casinos, and other businesses around Miami. Each time a traveler would step outside the airport and get into the car waiting for them, the long line of vehicles would move one stall to the right so that another car could get in closer to the door.

A memory came to me of my brother driving a taxicab in New York; he was okay. But this was Miami; he had just moved there a few months ago. I had forgotten to ask him what kind of car he was driving. Would he find me? Suddenly every driver seemed to look like my brother. I hadn't seen him for a while, and my stressed mind played a trick: I forgot about his looks for a moment.

Then I heard a horn. I turned around to see an older red Cadillac moving slowly toward me. "That can't be him," I said to myself. But the horn kept honking, and I looked again—it was Estephan. He stepped out of the car, and we went straight toward each other with our arms open wide. We whispered a few words to each other, "We do not have a father anymore." For a brief time, neither of us knew what to say. Estephan opened his car's trunk and helped me load my heavy suitcase. I sat in front while he positioned himself to start the vehicle.

My brother lived in Fort Lauderdale, Florida, about twenty-five minutes from Miami International Airport. He asked me why I did not try to land five minutes away from his house at the other international airport. I explained that the ticket would have cost me an extra $100, which I did not want to spend. I tried to save as much money as possible because I did not know how to be responsible for the funeral costs. The thought flowed through my mind that I did not know what to say to him.

On the drive to my brother's house, I saw some palm trees, and they reminded me that I was getting closer to the Caribbean. After leaving Nebraska in single-digit temperatures, driving around in sixty-degree weather was a welcome change.

As we got close to his house, one of the standard traveling rules (for me, anyway) occurred: Never go to Haiti without Ibuprofen. It was almost after midnight. So, I told Estephan, "Please, let's find a twenty-four-hour store so I can get some medicine." So, we found a store two blocks later, and I purchased a bottle of Ibuprofen and a box of Zantac. You cannot live without those things when going to Haiti, and I kept saying to him.

I also wanted some extra cash, so I went to an ATM. I first confirmed my checking account balance, and it showed zero. I panicked a little. I knew that I had just deposited money in the bank, so I tried to calm down and think things through. I knew it usually takes a while before the ATM catches up with the actual bank balance, mostly if I deposited the money on a Friday afternoon. I calmed myself and realized that I would have to wait until Monday morning to have my wife recheck the balance over the Internet, and hopefully, everything would be fine. If everything were all right, I would have her transfer the cash via Western Union.

We discussed travel plans and how long we intended to stay in Haiti. Back in the car, my brother started to drive immediately. I reached to my right side to find the seat belt as he cleared the entrance to the parking lot. He turned on the radio. A soft but lively beat of a familiar tune was playing; Haiti's sweet, folkloric rhythm was the unmistakable sound.

Twenty-five minutes later, we arrived at what I thought looked like a retirement community. According to Estephan, the duplexes were part of an association that required the owner to pay an additional $130 monthly dues for upkeep. Coming from Nebraska, where we usually take care of our lawns, this arrangement sounded quite different from what I knew. Most houses were genuinely lovely, except they did not have basements.

My brother parked his car and helped me with my luggage. We went into his home, a lovely three-bedroom split-level house with a cathedral ceiling. The landing looked straight down into the living room. This house matched the type of home my daughter Rachel always bragged about owning someday.

When we entered the first room, my brother asked me to remove my shoes before climbing the stairs. Then he showed me his lovely room with an extended king-size bed. The headboard measured the whole room's length with bookcases, mirrors, and shelves to display figurines and other things.

We sat on the bed and discussed our plane reservations and travel plans. After some time, we realized it was almost three in the morning, and there was no way we would find time to sleep. It also occurred to both of us that we were hungry. Therefore, we decided to go and hunt for food.

We hopped in the car and headed straight for the nearest Denny's.

After parking the car, we walked into the restaurant. A friendly waitress escorted us to our seats. We talked about personal matters, including that Estephan was not entirely happy with his marriage. I kept telling him most unions have problems, but from what he told me, I believed that his situation, though not unique, would require him to make serious decisions.

The beautiful waitress who seated us came by to take our order. She was a charming Jamaican girl, had short, well-done hair, and did not have any trouble returning my brother's casual, harmless flirtation. My brother did not waste any time being extra friendly with her.

I had eggs, and my brother had a special omelet. While we ate, we convinced each other that it would be best for us to travel to Haiti simultaneously. As we talked, I noticed Estephan was wearing at least four rings. One of the calls was a gold horseshoe with a horse head on top. I told him it was a beautiful ring (horses are my favorite animals). He removed it and let me put it on my little left-hand finger, and it felt great.

Estephan said, "It's yours if you give me one hundred bucks." He said he had paid over $360 for it.

"Why would I want to pay you any money now? We all are going to need money."

He said, "That's right; I could use the extra cash."

We joked around about the price, and I kept the ring with a promise to pay him $100 later.

Back at my brother's house, we called the travel agent and several car rental places, and at about 4:30, we were ready to hit the airport.

My brother had not previously arranged for anyone to take him to the airport. Consequently, regrettably, we realized that the only way we would get there was to summon his wife's help.

She was a complicated driver. One minute we were traveling at the speed limit, the next minute, she would be flying at eighty-five miles an hour. I had to request more than once for her to slow down. At that point, I was desperately looking for my seat belt. According to some people at the time, I had an unusual habit: I never traveled in a car without having my seatbelt clicked. You need to understand; that this was before Nebraska law mandated seatbelt use, and somehow when I tried to explain this habit to others, I would find myself apologizing for it. But I had seen too many people get hurt because they didn't wear a seatbelt.

I tried to doze off despite driving on the way to the airport. Maybe I did because my brother reminded me later of my loud snore.

We arrived at the airport on time; however, finding a place to park and unload the car was another story.

Since we couldn't find a place to park, Estephan and I decided to brave the dense airport traffic, and we stepped out of the car while his wife was still in the middle of the road. We had two huge buses beside us trying to get into our lane. My sister-in-law, our fantastic driver, had to use one of those bicycle bungee cords to hold the trunk of her car in place because someone had rear-ended the vehicle a few months back. We unloaded as quickly as possible, grabbing our suitcases and putting the cord back in place before some nut driver could get out of their car to strangle us. Finally, we made it safely inside the airport.

The line at the ticket counter to go to Haiti was exceedingly long. One of the Haitians in line asked us whether it was all right that someone else had paid him money so that he could check luggage for that person. I told him it was illegal and wanted to stay out of it. They had a mobile security station to check luggage before checking in at the regular counter. The security guard also asked me for the laptop I was carrying on my left shoulder. Finally, it was my turn to hand over my bags, and I noticed how badly they treated these suitcases; I hesitated before turning mine over.

I said, "Oh no, you're not going to get this one; this is my computer, and nobody touches it."

He looked at me strangely and said, "Okay, go ahead; this was pre-September 11.

We arrived at the counter after what seemed like an hour. We handed over our credit cards and paid for our tickets.

We had close to an hour to kill before the flight to Haiti.

I used the time to go to the bathroom and look around the airport before going to our gate. The plane was a 747, and our seats were close to an exit door. My brother joked with the flight attendant, saying, just because you put us by the exit door, do not expect us to help anyone if there is a problem.

I had forgotten how international flights and domestic flights were different. This American Airlines plane had three rows of seats. Above the middle seats, some television screens dropped down and retracted as needed. They used them for entertainment and to give security directions. They also provided a headset to listen to more than twelve different radio channels of your choice.

Haiti is six hundred and thirty-one miles from Miami; the flight took one hour and forty-five minutes. The flight was relatively smooth. Estephan and I were tired because we hadn't slept well since the news of our father's death and then stayed up half the night talking. We tried to nap but woke up suddenly when the flight attendants handed out immigration papers and distributed food and drink.

Chapter 34

Arrival in Port-au-Prince

When we arrived in Haiti, the sun was shining, and the temperature was in the seventies. The Haiti airport does not have an indoor gate to get from the airplane to the airport. Instead, they have stairs from the aircraft to the ground, and travelers walk to the airport. Our flight had at least seven hundred people. One group stepped down from the front of the aircraft, and another from the rear.

Estephan and I were in the rear group. The stairs were steep going down, and some people were trying to get ahead of us as we went. I saw a huge sign saying International Airport of Haiti in English and French. We could see the black text on the character since the colors of the building were light fluorescent green and beige.

Five rows were going into immigration.

We were way at the back of the line. Suddenly one of the immigration officers said to Estephan, "Phillip, you should not be so far behind. Give me your passports and come in." He was a friend of my brother's. I was stunned, and everyone around looked at us as we went into the immigration area.

We were among the first ones inside, and we didn't have to stand before an immigration officer. We gave my brother's friend our passports and the papers we had filled out on the airplane, and he took them to the immigration officer working in the booth. A few minutes later, he returned our passports to us. We talked to him for a while, and Estephan spoke to other people he knew who showed up. I didn't see anyone that I recognized. I had become a stranger after twenty-three years.

The Port-au-Prince airport had a long S-shaped conveyor belt in one baggage claim area. That was also where everyone congregated after passing through immigration. Estephan and I waited for our suitcases, and, luckily, we found them in no time and headed straight outside.

One thing I never got used to in Haiti was the thousands of people waiting outside the airport to help travelers with their luggage.

Thankfully, I spotted my brother Benjamin over the fence.

Benjamin was a well-respected Jehovah's Witness and one of the deacons in his church. Among all my brothers, he was the one I could sit down and talk with for hours without any confrontation or argument. I could almost do the same thing with my brother Estephan because of his maturity. But Estephan and I have different tastes in life, while Benjamin and I have the same taste in almost everything except that I would never become a Jehovah's Witness.

I gave my suitcase to Benjamin, and we exchanged a firm embrace. He was driving my father's Jeep, and I told him to wait while I went to Hertz for a car. I knew we needed an extra vehicle because several family members had yet to fly in. My sister Melissa, whom I hadn't seen for twenty-three years, was coming from Paris. My brother Gerard, sister Veronica, and son Gregory came from New York. And my brother Gabriel was coming from Lincoln.

I could not find a car at Hertz immediately, so we boarded the Jeep.

The streets were incredibly dusty in Haiti, and because of the road construction going on everywhere and all the time, there were constant traffic jams. The exhaust fumes from the standing traffic and road dust made the air pollution about one hundred times greater than anywhere I had been before. One day of breathing that dust was enough to take you straight to the hospital.

During the previous few years, Haiti's new government had tried to make some positive changes in infrastructure; however, it was tough to see these changes because of the country's extreme conditions (and maybe all the dust).

When I left Haiti twenty-three years ago, some of the things they called changes were things the country had had before and that we took for granted. We knew what we had when they took away these things, but it was too late. Now the government was giving them back and making a big deal.

Chapter 35

Arrival at My Mom's House

After a long journey home, we finally arrived at my mom's house. Naturally, I went straight to see her.

When someone dies in Haiti, people make a lot of noise: they scream, they cry. As soon as my mom and sister saw me, they started to weep loudly. My mom and I embraced as I tried to hold her; her body shook, screaming her heart out.

My mom did not know Estephan would come with me, and she did not immediately see him because her sight was terrible. She turned around, saw Estephan, and repeated the same process.

The screaming was getting louder and louder. Now the screaming came from other family members: Natasha, my sister; Lozanne, my dad's sister; and other people I could not immediately identify. We all cried for a while and then sat and talked for a long time.

I was dying to find an isolated place to work on my computer. My parent's house was a two-story cement house with four bedrooms, a vast, open area upstairs, a bathroom, and a small sun porch. I located the northwest bedroom upstairs, which was approximately a four-by-eight-foot room. Though small, it served the purpose of what I wanted to do. It had a key lock, a small bed, a wooden cabinet, and a small table where I could set up my computer. I installed a fan on a wall shelf, which I wanted.

You must understand that I have always been a quiet man; there were many people. It was hot and humid, and they talked a lot. Privacy was out of the question.

We had access to electricity about once a day for two to six hours, depending on the times of the electric company's scheduled blackouts. I spent a few hours working on work and my website.

Chapter 36

Saturday Evening

On the following Saturday evening, January 6, I walked into the hall of my parents' house and talked with some people, apparently friends of the family I did not know. One of them was a policeman, and he had about twenty to thirty driver's licenses in his pocket that he had confiscated that day.

He told us stories about corrupt cops who would stop people for no reason. Once, a policeman confiscated Benjamin's license plate from his car, and it took Benjamin a long while to get it back. Another policeman had stopped a person for an alleged traffic violation; instead of ticketing the driver, the policeman sat in the passenger seat and said, "You know why I am here," meaning he wanted the driver to give him money.

There were some things I wanted to do for my family while I was in Haiti, and I knew that I would not be able to do anything for the funeral until Monday morning. So, I gathered everyone together that Saturday night and explained my plan. I also told them that Gabriel would arrive on Monday from Nebraska, Veronica, Gregory, and Gerard on Tuesday, and Melissa on Thursday.

I had planned to go to the funeral home with the family on Monday morning, January 8. As a result, that morning, my mom, Natasha, Estephan, Benjamin, and I took Dad's Jeep and went to the funeral home. My dad's brother Lucien also went with us.

The funeral home was next to an old school I had attended in Haiti in 1975 and 1976, Lycee Toussaint Louverture. They named the school after a Haitian revolutionary hero. The funeral home was about two blocks north of the Catholic Church where my dad had requested to have his funeral at—St. Anne's.

Chapter 37

At the Funeral Home

After going up one ramp and a few stairs, we arrived at what seemed like an electric gate. There was a very tall iron gate on the funeral home's west side; the entry had a pink-and-white mosaic floor. A receptionist in a box-like office guarded it. We talked with her, and she pushed a button to let us through the door. The atmosphere was more like going to a state prison than a funeral home.

We climbed narrow stairs shaped like a spiral staircase, with carpet badly needed repair. Finally, we arrived at a wood-and-glass door after the third flight of stairs. On the left, we saw a middle-aged secretary. She could have used a lesson or two in customer service; during the first half-hour we were there, she maintained a stone-faced expression. Two or three other families were waiting ahead of us. Benjamin and I talked with the secretary, and they told us we needed to wait. So, we sat patiently on the bench to wait.

We noticed another door with a bell behind the secretary's desk. On more than one occasion, we saw people coming in, ringing the bell, and going through the door. The secretary had three chairs in front of her desk, and at one point, two people came and, without waiting, sat down in them, discussing funeral arrangements, we supposed.

At first, the secretary did not know, and my brother Estephan was impatient.

Estephan sat in one of the chairs in front of the secretary's desk. We were waiting for our turn. Benjamin and I signaled to Estephan that we had already talked to her. Benjamin had lived with my dad; he knew the funeral process and was also in contact with a gentleman who worked at the funeral home named Frankel. Frankel was related to my half-sister Melissa who lived in Paris, so we thought he would take care of things properly.

When they finally got to us, the secretary sent us through the secret door with the bell. I was expecting something different than what we found. As soon as we opened the door, we noticed an accountant working with a family through a glass door. In the main room, there were three desks where two workers and the funeral home director sat. The worker on the right told us to come in and sit at her desk. Benjamin and I sat in front of her desk on the two chairs available, and the rest of the family sat in the west corner on the right side of the funeral home director's desk.

The funeral parlor had done everything by hand. There was no computer, and the worker seemed only partially organized. We waited as we allowed her time to remove the previously completed documents from her desk. She had difficulty finding our record until Benjamin pointed it out to her. As she looked at it, Benjamin told her that we had been working with Frankel and wanted Frankel to be there so that we could complete the transaction.

Chapter 38

Showroom

The worker asked a few questions and then took us to the funeral home's showroom, where we could choose a casket for my dad.

When we arrived at the showroom, we could see ten to twelve Casket s. On one side was the imported Casket s, nicely decorated. Two were brown, two silver, and the other sky blue. On the opposite side were some tiny Casket s and a few handmade ones. The clerk asked us to choose, and we picked an imported brown casket. Then we went back to the room where we had been before to talk prices.

The worker wrote a few things on her tablet and showed us a price of $17,750. Meaning $3,800 compared to the U.S. rate of exchange at the time. The value of the U.S. dollar in Haiti was almost four times that of the Haitian dollar. Unfortunately, I hadn't talked to the rest of the family about how we would pay the funeral costs. I thought I would have to pay for the whole thing myself. I tried to bargain, but the worker refused and only trimmed the price to about $17,000 Haitian.

We came out of the secret room. Now it was time to fill out the other required papers. First, we provided the funeral home with family members' names we wanted the radio and newspaper announcements to include. I wrote down some words, and Estephan completed the list and turned it over to the secretary to type. The funeral home workers warned us not to list too many names because the newspaper would likely not include them.

We went home a bit bewildered.

I decided to wait until Veronica arrived from New York to have a family meeting and determine how much everyone could contribute to the funeral cost. I didn't particularly appreciate concentrating on the money, but it was practical and necessary.

Chapter 39

Eve of the funeral

On Monday afternoon, Gabriel was supposed to arrive from Nebraska. Benjamin and Nono, a cousin, went to the airport to get Gabriel. He was supposed to arrive at 3:30 p.m. At 5 p.m., I called his house to find out what was happening, and his wife assured me that he had left Nebraska. I also talked to my wife, who confirmed that Gabriel had picked up an air mattress at our home in Elkhorn that I had forgotten to bring with me before leaving.

I had not heard any calamity in the news; I concluded that Gabriel had missed his flight and assured myself that he would catch the next one and probably arrive Tuesday morning, January 9.

Tuesday was going to be a hectic day. We were supposed to pick up three people at the airport in the afternoon, now that we assumed that Gabriel would make it on that morning's flight. Benjamin had a friend who worked at the airport, and the friend promised us that he would keep an eye on the passenger list for us and call if he saw a Phillip on the list.

We sent a group of people to the airport in the morning and kept another person on standby to go to the airport in the afternoon to receive the family members arriving from New York.

Thankfully, Gabriel did make it on Tuesday morning. Unfortunately, my assumption was correct; he had missed his flight and had to stay at a motel in Miami.

The group from New York arrived at the house around 6 p.m. At about 8 p.m., I gathered everyone for a quick family meeting. We gathered in the room where my dad used to sleep. Space inspired a great deal of nostalgia and emotion. My dad had been in bed in that room for three years. Before leaving the country, the children and wife had not been in the same room together since 1978.

I talked to everyone, explained my plan, and made a plea for the funeral's financial contributions. Veronica said she would give me $600 and send me more when she returned to the U.S. Estephan said he would charge $500 on his credit card. Gabriel said he should have transmitted the money instead of coming to Haiti and used all the cash available to stay at the motel in Miami. Gerard said that he would give me $50.

I told everyone not to worry about the money if it was a burden to them and that things were more important than any financial contribution. Natasha had been caring for my dad for the last three years that he had been bedridden. Her actions were worth much more than any money could buy. My mom, Benjamin, and other family members contributed more than we who lived overseas could have ever done.

We talked about some other things during that meeting as well.

Estephan wanted to ensure that my dad's name did not fade away, especially at the auto repair shop he had spent most of his life building. Unfortunately, he passed away in March 2000. Unfortunately, during the last three years, the shop has lost some vital members, especially Pierre Richard, who had been in charge while my dad was ill. Thankfully, Marius, a man who had been with my dad for as long as I could remember, had two sons working at the shop, so it seemed like it was in good hands. However, as we discussed the shop and what to do, I thought that it was unfortunate that none of my dad's sons, for various reasons, had been able to work there.

Estephan wanted to save the location since real estate was scarce in Haiti and wanted to talk to Athea, the landowner, about this. He also felt we should instruct the shop people to proceed since my dad was no longer around. I felt both these things were necessary but could not see how I could handle that and the funeral matters. So, I asked Estephan to oversee the shop, and he later set up meetings with the shop workers and took my brothers to talk with them.

After everyone explained what they could contribute, I had a better idea of proceeding. But unfortunately, Melissa had not arrived yet. Since I hadn't seen her for twenty-three years and had no idea what she could offer, I moved with the understanding that I might not receive any financial contribution from her. So, I called my wife and instructed her to transfer some money. She shared $1,000, so I had enough on my credit card to cover the rest of the funeral costs if it came to that point. Later, when Melissa arrived from Paris, she gave me $500 to help cover the funeral, for which I was grateful.

I intended to use the air mattress that I had asked my wife to send with Gabriel to sleep that night. Unfortunately, I couldn't use it because we lost the lid when I tried to set it up. When Gabriel came by later, he said he had been working, and we did not need the cover. We tried with mine, and nothing worked. There was a slight complication in the overall picture, but the air mattress would have been excellent.

I then headed to the bank to get the Western Union transfer—for the second time. The first time I went, the money had not arrived. Haiti has some friendly banks: clean and air-conditioned by armed private security guards. While waiting in line, I attempted to call the U.S. about the money transfer on a cell phone I had borrowed since my cell had no service there. A female security guard came over and asked me not to use the phone. She apologized and explained that it was for my safety.

"I know that you do not look like a thief, but thieves could get in here, call other gang members outside, and give them specific information about what you're wearing so they can rob you when you leave," she said. Benjamin told her that my phone call was going to the U.S. to obtain information about the money transfer and that she had nothing to fear. Unfortunately, this reassurance did not help much with this bank policy.

Chapter 40

Wednesday—Hertz

I wanted to go to the funeral home on Wednesday but had no car access. However, I had noticed that Gabriel's friend Junior from Nebraska, who also came to be with us, had a nice car, so I asked him to take us to Hertz to get my rental, and he agreed, and we got ready to go.

Gabriel sat in the front seat so that he could talk with Junior. As I got into the car, we noticed a flat tire.

So junior and Gabriel went to change the tire while I waited. I remained for a long time, and they never showed up.

I immediately invited Gregory and Benjamin to accompany me to the bank, where we ordered a cab. The taxi driver cost us roughly $20 Haitian to transport us to Hertz near the airport.

The trip took a long time. It seemed longer because it was hot, the taxi was not air-conditioned, and you could not roll up the windows to keep the ever-present road construction dust out. The construction dust was flying all over, and they were trash throughout the whole area. It smelled like we were going to a garbage dump. Every road we drove on needed repair—counting the number of potholes was impossible. The owners of most of these vehicles on the street should have hauled them to a car cemetery so they could crunch them. They had numerous dents, scrapes, and various pieces of metal welded together; these were not cars, they were scrap metal with wheels, and some were expensive.

I was surprised when my brother would point to a situation where someone could get ticketed by the police, and I tried very hard to understand why it was a traffic violation—because it all seemed like chaos to me. There were no traffic lanes or traffic signals. Drivers played chicken with other drivers, speeding up to pass and slamming on the brakes when they couldn't, driving around cars (maybe there was a reason the security guards stopped the vehicle, perhaps not), and following no clear rules of the road. I had no idea whether two cars would collide until they had finished passing each other.

There was a long traffic jam just a few miles from Hertz on the road to the city's airport. The government had hired a contractor to repair the road, and it looked like they were working ridiculously hard to complete it. But the traffic on the road made it difficult for construction, and it didn't look like they had enough equipment and qualified workers to get the job done well. Aristide's new government took over on February 7, and I understood that he had given them a deadline to finish the job before inauguration day. It did not look promising.

When we finally arrived at Hertz, we found that the entrance to their lot was almost impossible. There was a deep hole left in the road by the construction, and the slightest error in steering would put the car directly into it.

We spent almost an hour with one of the Hertz representatives. He took us to the lot to show us the cars that they had available. We agreed on a vehicle and were getting ready to pay when he dropped a bombshell. I've been on the road and have rented a car at least once a week; all I ever needed was my driver's license and credit card. I needed at least two types of identification, a "state driver's license, and a passport." I hadn't wanted to walk around with my passport, and I didn't bring it for this; I had forgotten I was in a foreign country.

After all the trouble I had gone through to get to Hertz, I now encountered the prospect of not getting a car. I pleaded with the representative to let us have the car. He brought another representative to whom we explained the situation, but it was hopeless. We even offered to have them hold our driver's licenses, so we could go and get my passport, but they refused. They insisted that we had to have our American Passports, or no car would leave the lot.

Chapter 41

Unforgettable Tax

The taxi driver said he would wait for us for about fifteen minutes. We thought everything would work out, and we told him he could leave—what a mistake.

We were near the airport, so finding an available taxi was like finding a needle in a haystack. We waited a long time and finally saw a cab with two passengers inside. The taxi driver told us he could take us, but he had to first drop off these people in Carrefour Clercine, about ten miles from the funeral home. Ten miles in Haiti is like fifty miles in the U.S. With the construction and the potholes, cars can only go ten to fifteen miles per hour.

Benjamin sat in front of the lady and the driver. Gregory and I sat in the back with the man.

From the way the two passengers talked to each other, they seemed like a couple, calling each other this and darling. I could see the back of the lady's head, and I noticed that her hair seemed extremely dirty, and the end of her neck had a couple of moles and a few powder-like white spots. I was unsure if this was because of the dust blowing into the car. Maybe it was the powder leftover from her makeup. I learned later from my brother that the white spots could have been ceremonial sprinkling during a voodoo ceremony from that morning.

Seven people in a small car were uncomfortable, and the wind blew the contaminated air into our faces.

I asked if I could roll up the window. The driver opened the glove compartment and passed the door handle to the man next to Gregory to give it to me. I tried to roll up the window, and the door handle fell on the floor. Since we sat so close to one another like sardines, I could not reach down to retrieve it. I kept thinking, "I am doomed, I am doomed," with every bump we encountered on the road. I started having problems breathing, and my head began to ache—a considerable headache was on its way. I began coughing and realized that the dust had triggered my asthma.

After hours, the taxi dropped off the couple, and Benjamin asked me to get in front. As we moved forward into traffic, other people walking by the road asked to get into the taxi. I said to the driver, please do not stop for anyone else. He joked about my size and said he would never attempt to put someone else next to me. I had never appreciated being big before. I thought, thank God, I am a fat man!

On our way to the funeral home, we saw some strange accidents. One truck blocked the road because its chassis had broken in two. Another big truck almost backed into us as the driver tried to avoid a considerable bump and pothole.

The taxi finally dropped us off at the funeral home a few hours later. My hair was yellow with dirt; I was miserable, coughing, and sick to my stomach. Nevertheless, I kept saying, "I do not care how much it costs; I will get myself a car—with air conditioning."

We went to the restroom to remove the dirt from our heads. Gregory spent a little more time in the bathroom because he had accidentally stepped into a pile of mud running after the taxi at Hertz. There was mud all over his brand-new Nike.

Chapter 42

Money-Saving Tricks

I returned to the funeral home to purchase a less expensive coffin. Frankel, who was there this time, had the same thought and intended to urge us to choose a less expensive casket for reasons other than financial savings.

"Why do you believe we should give our father less than he deserves?" I questioned Frankel. "Have you gone to the graveyard recently?" he said. Of course, I'd been to the graveyard several times. Then he told us terrifying stories about cemeteries. He noted that some keep an eye on funerals. They're looking for over-decorated caskets. They would return after everyone had left to empty the coffin of all precious decorations.

Some of these vandalisms are the results of instructions from the funeral home. They frequently employ these guys to do these horrific types of heresies. They may even dispose of the body and take the coffin. He advised me to purchase a specific type of casket lock with a key given back to me to ensure that no one disturbed my father's burial.

After I heard about such a horrible fate that could occur, I got even sadder as I completed the preparation for my father's burial. My heart has gotten more troubled. For a brief moment, I was unsure whether I was grieving my father's loss or sad about the ever-growing misery that the country itself had to endure.

Driving by the cemetery, I saw people standing or sitting with their backs against the cement fence. For the first time, I began to question the real reason they were there. Were they there to beg for money, or were they agents hired to commit crimes against those genuinely gone from this world?

Chapter 43

Unexpected Disappointments

Before he had become bedridden, my dad had purchased a cemetery plot five- or six years prior. As we call them, he had built his cave, or mausoleums, as known in the US. They make them out of cement blocks with four chambers covered with light green mosaic tile. On top of the cave was a space to put ornaments and pictures. A one-foot white privacy fence on top surrounded the upper portion of the cave, and a wall of mortar and a small black iron door with a padlock secured each chamber. My father had spent a considerable amount of time while he was alive building that cave and decorating it the way he wanted.

Frankel explained there was a continual problem with people breaking into caves at night to steal ornaments from caskets. The thieves would remove the casket handles, dump the body onto the ground, and steal it if the coffins were in marketable shape enough. He told us several stories about this in gruesome detail.

I could confirm his stories. When I went to the cemetery, I walked by several caves and saw people had vandalized them. You could look at the holes punched through the entrances and, sometimes, bones lying beside the cave, thrown around like a horror movie scene.

Scattered throughout the cemetery were broken casket parts, and it looked like Dracula's town. I was distraught and disgusted when I took a shortcut to my dad's cave and could smell the stench of a broken casket about five hundred feet from it.

My dad's tomb was in a secure area, and it did not look like anyone could break into it, but I talked to the security guard about it anyway. He assured me that the cemetery security had been trying their best to correct the situation and had asked people to do more to secure their plots, as my dad had done. Unfortunately, most people did nothing, which, of course, helped the thieves.

Chapter 44

Negotiating Table

Back at the negotiating table, I could have the funeral home reduce the funeral price to $10,000 Haitian exchange value or 50,000 gourds. But instead, we watched in wonder and amusement as the secretary took the whiteout and erased the contract's previous amount. Working with computers daily, I had forgotten how things used to be before they were around.

Benjamin and I left the funeral home feeling that we had accomplished something. Finally, we would get the same package deal, a funeral with fanfare and video for our dad at a much more reasonable price.

Chapter 45

Crucial Phone Call

When we got back to my mom's house, I tried desperately to find a phone in the area to call my wife back in the U.S. Unfortunately, the owner of the cell phone I had borrowed took it back.

Most regular landline phones in Haiti did not work. The government had made it almost impossible for people to use a standard telephone, forcing them to purchase a calling card for long-distance calls. The calling cards cost about $20 Haitian; when you called the U.S. with them, you were only allowed between four and six minutes.

Teleco was the primary telephone company in Haiti; if anyone had a phone I could use, surely it would be them. I decided to go to the Teleco office downtown to see if they could use a phone for a long-distance call. When I walked in, I noticed most of the counters were empty, and only one person was working. I asked him for a phone, and he said no phone was working there. I would have to buy a calling card. He showed us the phone card, saying we were supposed to pay 100 gourds, then be charged an additional ten gourds for a fee.

Of course, I could not use a phone inside the Teleco building. So, I had to use an outside payphone. He said there should be one by the Market (the Haitian version of a Kwik Shop-type store).

Benjamin and Gregory went inside the Market since it was air-conditioned, and I got in line outside and waited. Outside the Market, at least six or seven people were waiting in line to use the pay phone. When it was finally my turn, the card instructed me to dial 1-0-3 and 0-0-1, the number I wanted to call. Each time I dialed 1-0-3, the phone was busy, or an operator came on the line to tell me that I would have to try my call later.

After the twenty-third time, I got through, though I quickly realized that I would burn through my four minutes faster than I had expected because I put some restrictions on my phone in the U.S. to avoid telemarketers. When unidentified callers phone my house, they must identify themselves before the call rings through to the phone. By the time I had gone through the operator in the U.S. to identify myself, I had used up about half of my $20 card. I finally got to the house phone, but no one was home. I left a message for my wife but did not wait to confirm it and later lost the note.

Chapter 46

Thursday Morning—Get a Car or Else

I was determined to get a car on Thursday morning, and I even slept with my passport next to me. So, Benjamin, Gregory, Benjamin's son Olivier, and I took a taxi and returned to Hertz. It took us almost the whole morning to get this done.

I noticed that if you make a reservation from the U.S. with Hertz the night before, you can sometimes get a better deal on a car rental. I finally reached my wife later Wednesday night and instructed her to make the reservation. When I arrived at the Hertz counter the following day, I gave them the reservation number, and luckily, they found my name on the reservation list. The price of the rental also dropped from $600 to $354.

Then the Hertz representative said they had a special that week, only $294 for a one-week rental. I knew there would be a catch to this, so I asked him to explain. The price he quoted me was without insurance. "You will need to pay ten dollars daily," he said. He did some fuzzy math and came up with $367. "Fine, get me the! @%$#%@ car and get me out here."

At that point, my credit card had no charges yet. I knew there would be an authorization for more than the actual amount, and they would adjust the cost once I returned the car. The approval that the representative made was for $1,000. I had no idea that it was going to be that much. He explained one more time the insurance and the deductible. Even though I was paying an extra $10 per day for insurance, my liability could go up to, but not exceed, $2,000. I asked myself, "Would this car be worth that much in the U.S.?" No. It was a white 1999 four-door Lancer with about twenty-six thousand miles. It could look a lot nicer in better road conditions.

I said, "Give me the key."

The representative photocopied my passport and driver's license, ran my credit card through his manual credit card processor, and asked me to wait. I waited for another hour. Finally, my patience was wearing very thin. Two hours after they processed my card, someone arrived with my car.

Benjamin, Gregory, and Olivier were already inside the car. We went outside to inspect the vehicle, and the car inspector took me around for the physical body damage evaluation. He held in his hand a piece of paper that contained a diagram. We walked around the vehicle to locate possible damages. He would mark the chart with a pen each time we found something.

Benjamin had been driving for me ever since I arrived in Haiti. After I got the car, his first comment was, "Go ahead and drive, Bob. I'm not going to drive this car." So, I sat in the driver's seat, turned the air conditioner on, and headed for the dusty gravel road.

I felt better because I finally had a car that would isolate me from the brutal environment.

We went back to my mother's house to pick up Estephan so he could use his credit card at the funeral home to pay for some of the expenses. Estephan said he would only charge $350, so I didn't have to pay him for the ring he gave me.

Sizing clothes for the burial

Two days before, we had given Frankel $10 to ensure that our chosen casket would fit into the cave. I had asked him what he needed the $10 for, and Frankel had explained that he would use the $10 to go and measure the casket and the cave. I said, "What kind of service am I getting for the $10,000 I'm paying the funeral home? Shouldn't everything be included in the cost?" It made me uneasy, and I suspected I would have to double-check everything.

There was a man named Milord whom my dad had hired to take care of his cave. Milord came over to talk to us later that day. He asked us to cut the grass around the cave, and I paid him $60, and he and I went to the cemetery.

In front of the cemetery, more than one hundred men were standing around. They made their living by asking people who came to the graveyard for money to care for their caves. We drove slowly through the crowd to the gate, where the security guards stopped us. Milord got out of the car to talk to them. He was given a laminated card to hang on our rear-view mirror and asked me to pay them the $6 entrance fee. I told the guards that we would pay them when we got back.

After a short drive, we arrived at my dad's cave. We measured the cave chamber entrance, about thirty inches wide and twenty-two-and-a-half inches tall. The casket we chose was about thirty inches wide and twenty-five inches tall.

I drove Milord back to my mom's house and went to talk to Estephan.

Estephan and I drove back to the funeral home, and the whole thing turned into an absolute nightmare. First, they told me that the body was too big and that none of the caskets we looked at, nor the one we had chosen, would work. Then, they told me we would have to settle for a handmade casket made from wood, and no one at the funeral home was inclined to let me know how this would affect the casket's cost. Finally, they showed us the handmade casket, which looked like a giant, ugly matchbox. Its dimensions were thirty-two inches wide and twenty-six inches tall, which meant it would not fit into the cave.

Now I have two different problems. First, we could not find a suitable casket big enough for my dad, and even if we did find one, we would have to face the expense of modifying the tomb to fit.

But why was I worrying about all these things? I was paying a funeral parlor to take care of a funeral, yet I was the one measuring the cave and the casket to be sure they would work. We had only a day and a half left before the funeral and had not done anything yet. I was becoming furious and could feel my blood pressure rising. I asked to see the funeral home director.

The director hadn't been involved with our funeral before, and once they explained things to him, he started to get very loud with his people. He used a walkie-talkie to reach Frankel, who, I presumed, must have been at the cemetery taking care of a different funeral. The director kept asking Frankel to find a phone to call him because the distance between the two walkie-talkies was too long, and the connection was not good. The director repeatedly said, "Frankel, please find a phone to discuss the Phillip family's emergency. Do you copy? I do not want to discuss this matter over the air. Please find a phone. Do you copy? Tell me where you are, Frankel." Frankel did not comply, and the director turned to us and said, "He's probably somewhere he isn't supposed to be."

The funeral director asked us to wait, and he would take care of everything. I told him that it should not be our concern that things didn't fit and that please do what was necessary to make it all work. I also said not to bother me any more about the cost, that $10,000 was what we agreed upon and no more, and that I did not want the terrible wooden casket they showed us.

Frankel returned to the funeral home shortly after that. I took him outside and bluntly explained the situation, and he assured me he would take care of everything. Meanwhile, Estephan and I waited for the director to tell us what he would do to remedy the situation.

After some time, the director returned upstairs to tell us they had taken care of everything. While we had been waiting, they had gone to the morgue with two different Casket s to physically try them out with the body. But unfortunately, only one of them would work, and the imported casket cost around $17,750.

They escorted us downstairs to the morgue, where we could see the body lying comfortably in the casket. I noticed that the funeral parlor workers had sprayed strong chemicals to help remove the smell. While looking around, I was astonished that the morgue's temperature gauges registered approximately 60 degrees Fahrenheit. I had expected a temperature of roughly 30 degrees. I am no expert in mortuary management, but I knew something was wrong.

I knew Haiti was having electrical problems, but this was too much. I asked the director and one of the workers about the high temperature, and they assured me that they had generators and everything was as it should be. I stayed only long enough to tell the director that we would take the imported casket and not pay any more than the agreed-upon $10,000. He assured me that we would not pay anything more.

Once we were upstairs, the secretary came into the room to talk to the director, saying they could not give us this casket for that price. The director reiterated his decision to the secretary, which ended the negotiation phase.

Estephan and I went to the accounting office, where I paid them 70 percent of the total, part of it in cash, and the rest charged to Estephan's credit card. We promised to return on Friday to pay the rest; we had to return to bring clothing for my dad's body.

Estephan and I went back to my mom's house, thinking this was the end of the nightmare. I drove several other family members to their homes and then moved to Benjamin's house to stay the night. Benjamin's private barber came over to do his hair. I asked the barber if he could give me a light trim, and he did a great job.

Chapter 47

Friday

After the first day or two in Haiti, I tended to stay at Benjamin's house instead of my mom's. I was mentally and physically exhausted most of the time, and it gave me a quiet place to rest while the hundreds of people who wished to share their family condolences stopped by my mother's house.

I was resting at Benjamin's house Friday afternoon when a messenger came by to tell me that Milord, the cave keeper, was looking for me. I rushed over to my mother's house to meet with him. Milord wanted to talk with me about how he would need more money for painting, cement, and other things to help make the cave more secure. We drove in my car to the cemetery to show me precisely what he planned to do to protect the Tomb, and I gave him some more money. I then drove him back to my mother's house.

It was now the day before the funeral, and I was exhausted. We needed to do only a few things before the funeral, but there would be no time to do them the next day with the visitation and viewing of the body at the funeral home at 6 a.m. and the church service at 7 a.m. However, I wanted the day to go by smoothly without any complications.

The night before, I had received some money from Melissa and Nolan, my cousin; I thought I would have to use my credit card to pay for the balance owed at the funeral. Still, thanks to my relatives' generosity, I didn't have to do that.

Once I returned from my mother's, Benjamin, and no one else, I went straight to the funeral home to pay the balance and give them dad's suit. We met a lady at the door and gave her the clothing. She asked us to come to the morgue to identify the body again and write letters certifying that this was our father's body. We thought this was odd—why couldn't they have already prepared something for us to sign?

We then went upstairs to pay, but the accountant was not available.

While we waited for the accountant, exchanging our U.S. dollars for Haitian money would be better. Then, perhaps we could get a better return.

In Haiti, thousands of young men do nothing but exchange money in the street to earn their living. As I found out, working with these people feels like dealing drugs; what we did could have been taken straight from a movie. We drove to a neighborhood where Benjamin claimed he knew people who could do the exchange. We stopped near a corner, and my brother got out of the car to look for a Person-to-person currency exchanger. A young man walked over to us, and I opened my car's back door so he could sit inside. We asked him how much money he had available for exchange, and he said he had about $4,000 Haitian. We needed $3,820 U.S. to pay the remaining balance for the funeral. I had about $1,000 in the U.S. In my possession, we offered him a little over $800, and the moneychanger offered us a bundle of money. Benjamin and the Person-to-person currency exchanger counted the bills carefully again and again. I gave the Person-to-person currency exchanger my cash while he handed me his; we simultaneously released our money from our hands. He then got out of the car, and I drove off. I had planned on turning around because it would be easier to go back the way we had come, but Benjamin suggested it would be better to go straight and take a different street. Neighborhood hooligans may have noticed the money exchange.

As I nervously drove the way he had indicated, Benjamin reassured me that he knew many hooligans and that it would be difficult for them to attempt to rob us. "Besides, all I must do," Benjamin added, "is mentioned a few names, and they'll leave us alone." Unfortunately, that did not make me feel any better.

I listened to my brother talk and drove without looking in the rearview mirror. I had begun to question the logic of going to a moneychanger in the street, jeopardizing us, to save a few bucks. But I also remembered that my other brothers occasionally exaggerated, and people exchanged money in the street without any problems.

When we returned to the funeral home, we went to the accounting office, found the accountant, and paid Haitian money. My brother Benjamin counted the money very carefully. Finally, the accountant gave us a receipt and marked our contract delivered in full.

Now that we had taken care of the funeral costs, we needed to go downtown to purchase some clothing articles we forgot to buy for dad. So, we drove downtown, and Benjamin went into the crowded market and returned with the clothing soon after.

We also wanted to copy Le Novelist's funeral announcement newspaper, one of Haiti's major newspapers. When we finally found a place that sold it, Benjamin went inside to get it and returned a little upset. The announcement failed to mention some crucial family members, such as Gabriel and Jayden. I asked Benjamin to get me a copy, and he returned with three. Later, Benjamin told me all his problems with the newspaper because they wanted him to pay more after publishing the announcement even though they had made many mistakes.

People began coming to the house later that night. It is customary in Haiti to have an all-night gathering the day before a funeral, but with all the trouble Haiti was having and the lack of electricity, my mother said she wouldn't have people stay the night. Instead, she told me she would start asking people to leave at 10 or 11 p.m. Besides, we had to get up at four in the morning to be at the funeral home in time to show the body.

The crowd started to come; I stayed with my mother until about 8 p.m., then went to Benjamin's house, thinking people would leave at about 10. At about 9 p.m., Gabriel came over to get Benjamin. All I could hear was a brief argument between Benjamin and Gabriel. Gabriel had stayed at the door and requested that Benjamin step outside to talk to him. Benjamin, in turn, asked Gabriel to come in, but Gabriel refused and left. I told Benjamin, "Maybe something is happening at the mother's house. Let's go over there and find out."

We found at least ten people surrounding my sister Melissa, who had difficulty breathing when we arrived. Something had caught in her throat, and she could not clear it with a cough. Someone had tried to give her water. Veronica attempted to massage the outside of Melissa's throat with her hand. Each time she did that, Melissa would choke even more. Finally, I asked Veronica to stop this nonsensical approach because it was not helping. Melissa was hyperventilating—crying and screaming—and I knew she had a cold. The weather and the house were sweltering, so I thought getting Melissa away from the crowd where she could relax would help her recover.

I asked Gabriel and Benjamin to bring Melissa to my car, and I drove her to Champ Mars, a genuinely lovely park near the palace. I gave her some Ibuprofen and asked whether she had asthma, and she said yes. She said she felt pressure in her lungs, so she could not breathe. I gave her a couple of puffs off my Primatene Mist, and a few minutes later, she felt better. I took her to Benjamin's house, and she slept for a while before someone took her back to my mother's house.

Someone came over later and told me that they couldn't control Estephan. First, Melissa cried without stopping; now, it was Estephan's turn. It was hot that night, and the mosquitoes had a banquet on my blood. I kept asking myself why I should go to bed when I would have to get up at 4 a.m. Finally, I asked Benjamin if he had an alarm clock, and he said not to worry about it; we would get up on time. So I went to bed and found myself waking every hour on the hour to check my watch: 1 a.m., 2:06 a.m., 3:20 a.m.

At 4:07, we heard someone honking outside. We thought maybe someone wanted to get us up. I looked out, but it was not anybody that we knew. I went to shower and get ready for the funeral. Everyone was already up when I got to my mother's house. We all kept saying variations of "this is the day."

There was already a crowd outside the house. So, to get everyone to the funeral home, we coordinated cars to drop off one group of people at the funeral home while a second or third car was coming back to get another group. I had the rented car, the family had the jeep, and a family friend brought a pickup truck.

Chapter 48

Funeral

At the funeral home that Saturday morning, I experienced one of the worst days as we said our final goodbye to our dad.

We had arrived early, and the funeral home workers did not have the casket ready for viewing. Consequently, we stood outside the panoramic glass room as they wheeled the casket inside. Then, as we do in Haiti, everyone started to scream, the men trying to hold back their grief, often with two or three of them trying desperately to hold up a screaming woman. It was the saddest thing that anyone could experience.

Veronica and Melissa slowly approached the casket. Veronica rubbed her hand on my dad's belly. She said, "I am talking to you; please answer me." She would turn around then and speak with sad confusion, "Why doesn't he answer me?"

It seemed like everyone was shaking and screaming uncontrollably.

At 6:10, the camera operators came in and started to take the video. We also had another member of my mother's family take photographs.

I could not sit down, and I wanted to do something. Benjamin had prepared a speech the night before, and I begged him to let me talk instead. I needed my dad to hear how thankful I was for what he had done for me. We agreed that I would start talking at about 6:15, and Benjamin would start his speech at about 6:30. I spoke to the cameraman and gave him instructions to turn down the music and turn the microphone on when we began to talk.

More people continued to come by, each stopping at the signing table outside the panoramic glass door. Then they would go inside, stop at the casket to pay their respects, and greet the family. Finally, so many people came in that I waited to begin my speech.

At 6:30, it was my turn to say something. I talked for a while and told everyone what I remembered about my dad. I had Benjamin stand by me, and I thought he would make the speech he had prepared the night before once I finished. Instead, he excused himself, saying it was too much for him. At 6:50, the brass band started to play, and everything broke loose. They were about to close the casket simultaneously, and everyone started screaming and crying again.

Once the casket was closed and prepared for the cemetery walk, many people escorted my mom and Melissa outside. I asked my mom if she wanted a ride to the cemetery, but she said she wanted to walk my dad to the cemetery.

We went on to the church. No one had told me that this would be multiple funerals, but when we arrived, I realized they were funerals for at least four other people and my dad. They do this as customary in Haiti; I just wished someone had told me. St. Anne is large and can accommodate many people, yet it is too crowded. There were thousands of mourners there.

We went inside, and those who were Jehovah's Witnesses stood outside. The cameraman was already inside, ready to take the video.

Chapter 49

Procession

After the service, which lasted an hour, everyone stepped outside to join the march to the cemetery.

One of the oddest sights I had ever seen caught my attention, and I continued to look at it until someone told me I needed to join the parade. I was shocked to see a bunch of workers struggling to mount a coffin on top of a big bus—a family who participated in the combined funeral needed to transport the body from Port-au-Prince to the countryside.

At the intersection of Rue Charreron, where my dad's business was, my dad's brother Lucien urged the hearse driver to halt the procession. The outcome was he believed that would have pleased my dad wherever he was. The driver did that, and when we stopped. Suddenly, I realized I did not know where my son Gilbert was. To find him, I dispatched someone to the head of the procession. When he returned, he informed me that Gilbert was in front of Gabriel and was perfectly safe.

The cemetery was our next stop.

Outside the cemetery, I got into another argument with the guards. My automobile was not allowed in, they said. I ran into a man I had previously spoken to, and I told him that my mother could not go that far and asked him to kindly allow the car in as she had become fatigued and gotten in the car. They eventually did, but by this time, the remainder of the walkers were far ahead of my automobile. They were waiting for Mom and me at the cemetery lot when I arrived before starting the burial. I pushed my way through the mob, and pardon me before getting to the location.

At the graveyard, Frankel and Milord were waiting for me. I gave them the go-ahead signal when they spotted me. We eventually managed to get the coffin. To observe what was going on, those at the back of the procession clambered onto other graves. Benjamin stayed with me as I waited at the cemetery until the workers had completed their work.

Before we departed, we checked to ensure Milord and his helper had erected the barrier properly. Milord and I had one last argument. His aide declined to mix the mortar with enough cement to form a solid connection. This type of dispute was becoming old to me.

To confirm that the gravedigger had done everything appropriately, I handed Milord an extra $30. I also instructed them to ensure everything was locked up before they departed.

I returned to my mother's house and began composing the chapters of this book. Benjamin escorted me to one of his friends' homes so I could finish my work once the power went off.

I was hacking and coughing that Saturday night. I felt dreadful. I had a head cold from the dust the entire time I was in Haiti, and the only things that appeared to help were four Ibuprofen tablets, some vitamin C Estephan had, and a glass of whiskey later—trying my best not to mix alcohol with medicine.

One whiskey bottle was for the family, and one was for me when Melissa arrived. The guys quickly consumed the second bottle after I handed my mother one to lock up.

On Friday night, Estephan had friends over and finished the second bottle. I went to Mom's house and asked her for the second bottle of whiskey since I felt like I could use that shot of whiskey. We don't have any more whiskey, my mother informed me.

In the hallway, Estephan was conversing with a few others. "You know, I don't like what you did," I told him. "You used the whisky that Melissa gave me as a gift without notifying me."

He said that Melissa did not gift it to you; she brought it for the occasion. Additionally, you don't drink. He said, "I drank it since the bottle would have stayed in the cabinet otherwise, which would have been a waste."

As family members do, we got into a bit more argument. I finally left and leaned against the power pole outside the beauty salon that Mom had rented. When he noticed me, Jayden emerged to speak with me. "You're acting exactly like Dad," he remarked. Same stance and everything when I look at you. Do not allow Estephan to cause you to become anxious for no reason.

I tried to rationalize my objection, "I don't mind if he drank the whiskey; I only ask that he have some manners. He should have admitted to drinking it, and I would accept it as a resolution to our conflict.

I had work to do at the apartment I rented to others. I called Gabriel in Lincoln and told him to meet me at TGI Friday to have a drink. After some lighthearted discussion between Gabriel and me, Gabriel proposed that I go out with him to Lincoln and get drunk while contacting my wife to inform her that I would stay the night there. Jaden stood by me.

He was exaggerating, and I do not remember this, but I did not pause to refute his story. I later explained to Estephan why I needed the whiskey.

I am not even an excellent social drinker, even though drinking has never been a passion or forbidden. I occasionally purchase beer that I store in the refrigerator for up to six months before consuming it. During my time in Haiti, I sometimes bought beer for drinking after meals.

I had sometimes taken a shot of Wild Turkey with tonic in the few months before the trip, but does that make me a drinker? I may love drinking since I'm a descendant of the Phillips bloodline, but I don't think I've ever gotten intoxicated in my entire life.

Then Estephan asked if I wanted him to get a new bottle; I replied, "Don't worry about it. "I'll make it," I said, and that was it.

The parade was a beautiful reminder of people's affection for my father. Despite his intimidating and challenging demeanor, he influenced many individuals. There were so many who came to show their respect. I often wonder if I might gain from such a remarkable benefit when I am gone.

Chapter 50

Sunday Dinner

I gave Benjamin's wife, Josephine, enough cash so she could make a final midday family luncheon on Sunday morning. I got up early that morning to write when it was still peaceful, and I could order my ideas.

Estephan and the other lads drove my dad's Jeep to see the acreage he had just bought. While they were away, Benjamin, his lovely wife Josephine, and I prepared the family dinner in the morning. My other brothers had already given Mom money to make their favorite dish, goat's head soup, when I went to my mother's house at around 9 a.m. to ensure the rest of the family would be present for supper. Mom promised me she would save the goat head for supper so everyone could eat at Benjamin's place that evening.

Veronica was conversing with Avaine, a family member I hadn't seen in a while, in the alleyway next to my mother's house. Avaine was three hundred pounds when I last saw him, but he was now only between one hundred sixty and one hundred seventy pounds and in good shape. I chatted with him while I sat next to him. He was describing to us how they handle funerals in the nation.

He joked that he wanted it sung at his funeral when he went away, making light of the fact that we weren't playing it. People would meet the day after the funeral, cook a ton of food, and have a party while drinking, playing cards, and singing.

You know what, I don't think I have the heart to celebrate my father's passing, I remarked. Make sure you tell your family before the celebration of your funeral if you want it.

Back at Benjamin's house, I continued to write there until the family arrived for a meal at approximately 12:30.

Benjamin and I arranged the tables. One of Benjamin's two long tables was higher than the other. The youngster needed food. He tried to prevent us from missing the legs because he believed it would take too long and sought a saw to chop the legs off the higher ones so the tables would match when Estephan came.

I went into the kitchen to keep Estephan occupied until supper and cooked him a salami sandwich. We asked if anybody wanted to assist Josephine in the kitchen. Instead of offering to assist, Veronica and Melissa entered the kitchen and helped themselves to some rice. The rice seemed incredible, I must admit; if I hadn't acted politely, I probably would have done the same. As opposed to waiting for everyone to sit and eat together, I made a joke with them and instructed them to go back to the dining room. Then, as Estephan leaned over to take a bite of the tempting chicken on the plate, I had to swat his hand.

Book Mark.....,

Gabriel reminded us how much dad would have wanted this; his dream was to have everyone together at the same table.

I ordered everyone to be quiet and reminded them that this was Benjamin's house and that he was in charge. Benjamin stood at the head of the table and asked everyone to bow their heads as he prayed. He paid homage to Dad and said a few things from the speech he had planned to give at the funeral. He asked us to observe a moment of silence. We then asked my mom to say a few words. She gave such an excellent speech; I was surprised at the depth of what she had to say about Dad. Dad's brother Lucien gave a short speech, and so did Natasha. Then Veronica said, "No more speaking—I want to eat now."

Later that afternoon, I went to my mother's house to talk with her before leaving. We talked about whether it was a good idea for Benjamin to move upstairs. Considering how private Benjamin was, he would probably not want to get involved with all the things in the house with Natasha and the other people currently living there.

That evening I chose to stay inside. It was Mardi Gras, and I could hear some bands playing in the street. Except for Benjamin, I believe my other brothers went out that night to party, but I have no idea where they went.

Chapter 51

Back to the U.S.

I scheduled my trip back to Miami for Monday, January 15, at 4:55 p.m. I was looking forward to seeing my wife and kids, Jo and Kathy, and the others at work.

We had been planning to bring my mom to the U.S. to stay with us. On Monday morning, we went to the American embassy. The embassy was not open. When I approached the doorman and gave him my passport so he could let us in, he said, "You are an American, and you don't know that today is Martin Luther King's birthday? You'll have to come back tomorrow."

I told him, "You have no idea what we've suffered here. The holiday in the U.S. is the last thing on my mind."

At that point, I had been in Haiti longer than any other, and I felt sicker and sicker the longer I stayed. Finally, Veronica, a U.S. citizen, wanted me to wait longer to go to the embassy with her and Mom the next day, and I told her she would have to take care of it unless I could change my flight.

I attempted that morning to find a phone to call and change my flight but was unsuccessful.

Benjamin, Olivier, and I then went back to the funeral home to pick up forms for everyone to give to their employers as proof of the funeral. The funeral home director was nice enough to have obtained names from us the day of the funeral, so we had one. We also wanted to pick up the video. The first time we went there, the forms were ready, but the video was not. They told us to come back at 9:30. We went to a restaurant in downtown Haiti near the palace to pass the time. We bought double burgers and took one to my mom. Once we were able to get the video, we went back to mom's house.

I talked to mom for a while and said an emotional goodbye.

Back on the plane to the U.S., Estephan and I had a chance to talk some more. We both realized the benefit of a family joint venture after what had happened with the funeral. All the Phillip kids could pull together their emotional and financial resources, and we took care of dad's funeral without difficulty.

I shared with Estephan the famous story about how strong a family can become when they stay together. I told him the story of a father who had three sons. The father gathered the sons one day and gave each one a small piece of wood while instructing them to break it.

Then the father took three pieces of wood, each the same size. He carefully wrapped a rope around them and made a knot at the end to keep the string from unraveling. Next, he gave each of his sons a bundle of sticks and ordered them to break it. The sons did not have any problem doing so. After several tries, they could not muster enough strength to break the bundle of sticks. Finally, the father said to them, "Be like the bundle of sticks. If you stay together, nothing can hurt you."

Estephan then shared a dream that my dad had shared with him. An exceedingly long ladder took people to an unknown destination in the sky. My dad, Estephan, and I were at the bottom of this ladder. However, each of us was attempting to climb it. Estephan and I had no difficulty climbing; however, he could not get to the top of the ladder no matter what Dad did. Sometime later, after this dream, my dad told Estephan to stick with me, that Estephan and I could do something with our lives.

I immediately told Estephan that my door was always open to come and be with me whenever he wanted to.

I do not know what it is, but most people prefer to be independent of their relatives. Kids usually can hardly wait to leave their parents to make their own decisions, and there are some benefits. In Haitian culture, being the firstborn, I am viewed as the father figure by the family, especially now that Dad has died. My brothers and sisters prefer to stay as far away from me as possible because they do not want me to interfere with their affairs or tell them what to do. Also, I remind them too much of our dad.

I often tell them that it depends on their ego level and how you deal with the natural order. Every tribe has a chief, every country has a head of state, every business has a boss, every family has a father, and the church has the Lord. I also believe that we have something unique that we can do that no one else can, but there needs to be organization and direction. Otherwise, you don't accomplish anything. During the last twenty-three years, I have been an employee and manager for some of the most reputable companies in the U.S., and I know how to give and take orders from others.

You are probably asking yourself, where is Bob going with this? Living in Nebraska has not been as easy for me as some think. I've experienced many business successes and many failures. I've seen families from China, India, and all other parts of the world assemble their resources, develop a business plan, and create successful enterprises.

When I see my four brothers, now scattered across the world, I imagine everything we could do if we were together. Granted, being apart has some benefits if the only goal your peace with your relatives has been. I am not suggesting that it would be smooth sailing if we ever got together to create a business, but the sky would be the limit with discipline and maturity.

When we arrived in Miami, I couldn't go to Estephan's house because he said he might not have time to bring me back to the airport the following day, and his work schedule was Tuesday morning. So, we said goodbye to each other.

I called a shuttle bus, and the driver took me to the Paramount Motel, about five minutes from the airport. Once at the motel, I called my wife and talked to my kids; I learned that Hannah had a slight cold and could empathize. I once more invoked my wife's expertise in locating information about my flight home. We found that I could change my flight for that afternoon, but it would cost an additional $75. I wanted to get home so badly, but for $75, I could wait. I called the front desk and asked for a wake-up call at 6 a.m.

I continued to work on this chapter with my dad and completed it while in the air over Chicago.

I hope that everything will work out well for my family, both here in the U.S. and abroad. I want to help Benjamin get to the U.S. as soon as possible; I feel it is essential. And I hope God blesses me to save enough money to cover my funeral expenses and spare my children the burden of such an extreme situation as my family and I have endured.

Chapter 52

2010 Earthquake

In January 2010, Haiti suffered one of the most devastating earthquakes. I went to the Island one week after that quake. From that trip, I started to add notes to the collection of my life memories. While reviewing these records, I observed a unique pattern that will help you read these lines.

If I can remember, people from Haiti have always been in pursuit of a better life. Unfortunately, young men who had finished high school had minimal options to secure a bright future. One could either become a doctor, a lawyer, or a teacher. The engineering and agronomy industries were also available, but very few youngsters could make a good living.

I first learned about the January 12th earthquake when I received a call from my wife. She was working at the Red Cross, and her co-workers had received an alert about Haiti. Later I also received a text message from my sister-in-law. It was the end of the day, and I was getting out of a meeting at work and getting ready to put my laptop away. I had no idea how serious this was until I got into my car and drove my usual 55-mile trip from work in Omaha, Nebraska, to my home in Syracuse.

When I turned the radio to CNN, my body went numb and started to penetrate my thick skull. I instantly sent a text message to family members and friends.

Words cannot describe how I felt at that moment of disaster in my homeland. Even though I have lived in the United States for 32 years and have been an American citizen for over 23 years, a part of my heart remains in Haiti as I still have family living there. That family includes my mother, one sister with five kids, grandkids, nieces, nephews, cousins, and second cousins.

As a grandfather, I usually do not like to answer the phone. Most of my relatives on my side of our family lived in New York; Fort Lauderdale, Florida; Paris, France; and Lincoln, Nebraska. My wife and I have children and grandkids scattered in Portland, Oregon; Tulsa, Oklahoma; Seward, Nebraska; and Omaha, Nebraska.

I never know whether the person on the other line will make me smile or add a few grayer hairs on my head with everyone so far apart.

As the magnitude of the crisis in Haiti began to permeate, I continued the drive home, staying within the speed limit but not fully aware of or caring about the distance I had traveled to get back. The most I could think about was getting there to turn on the TV and see the situation.

I was praying in an altered state of mind, like a trance. But all the same time, I was thinking, "Will praying do any good now? Whatever happened may have already happened."

As soon as I arrived home and saw the news media provided, I took calls to Port-au-Prince. But unfortunately, all I could get was a busy signal. My thoughts kept going back a few days to the night my wife and I watched the movie 2012. I kept saying, "This is the beginning of the end."

I called my sister in New York to discover whether other family members had talked to anyone in Haiti. Everyone was doing the same thing I was – calling, questioning, and hitting dead ends. Finally, we agreed that whoever got through first would let the rest of us know.

I spent the whole night glued to CNN and switching channels to find a glimmer of hope. Everyone was in a state of shock, and we felt helpless. I struggled with the thought that everyone was alive or had perished in the back of my mind. I was unsure if I should cry, scream, run away, or sit there and not do anything.

One heartwarming moment came when I called my boss at work. I was incredibly grateful that he understood. He assured me I could take as much time as needed to work through this emergency. He also asked that I let him know whatever he could do to help me. I am blessed to collaborate with such a man.

Since that afternoon, I have tried extremely hard to go through the motions of my daily activities. Decisions had to be made about the situation in Haiti and at home, and I was not 100% sure whether I was doing the right thing at the right time.

The earthquake had destroyed our house, and we did not yet know where any of our extended family members were. It wasn't until the second or the third day after the earthquake that one of my siblings finally got through by phone and talked to my mom. He called and assured us that most immediate family members were alive.

We owned a two-story house about 10 miles south of the national palace and less than one mile north of the Sanatorium Hospital in Port-au-Prince. I was about ten years of age when my dad built the first part of the house in 1965. It had only two rooms, a kitchen, a shower, and an outhouse. We made our home on half of the land we owned and used the other half as a playground.

In the early 70s, my dad added three more rooms: a living room, two bedrooms, and a porch. On a subsequent visit, I noticed he added a second story, and it contained a complete modern bathroom, a small patio, and four more bedrooms.

Houses are not built the same way in Haiti as in the U.S. Not every home has the luxury of facing the street. There were two houses west of us, one big house on the east, and countless other tiny homes on the south and north.

The main street, Rue Mon Seigneur, is on the east side of the house; a small alley leads back to the house.

I do not believe we built the house's first floor with enough strength to support such a significant structure. The earthquake crushed the bottom part of the house, and the upper portion stayed pretty much intact with some cracks. The top part of the building got tipped toward the north.

Ten kids live in the house with my sister and my mother. My mother was upstairs before the earthquake; she was partially blind and had other health issues. There were two kids inside with my mother when the quake occurred. The two kids got out through small holes in the rubble and went down an outside staircase leaning against the north neighbor's wall. One of the kids crawled back through a tiny hole to go after grandma.

Since she was partially blind, she was not fully aware of the gravity of the situation. The boy took her hand and slowly helped her climb through a hole. Minutes after they got out, the top of the house fell in, crushing the bottom part entirely. My mom and the boy got out without a scratch. The second child inside had several bruises on her legs, arms, and back.

Before the quake, my youngest sister had left the house for a cyber-café. She wanted to charge her phone and make a phone call to the U.S. Unfortunately, that café collapsed around her. She managed to get out of the building as it came down. But as soon as she got out, she fell, and in the panic, several people trampled over her, trying to get away. She broke her left wrist, and she had many bruises and scrapes.

We later found out that the husband of one of my nieces had lost his life downtown. She had a six-month-old baby. I was still in shock but was relieved to know that most of my family was all right. Unfortunately, I also learned the quake had injured several of my relatives. I was still scared, not knowing the extent of their injuries.

Haiti's locations had aftershocks every day, and no one could sleep inside due to fear of more buildings collapsing. Most of my family's belongings were still inside the crushed house, and they did not have much to sleep. So, neighbors brought them some blankets, and they slept in the yard.

I watched the news with a passion every day and prayed to find a way to go to Haiti. My family and I were frantic. Finally, my wife, who worked for the American Red Cross, began calling and writing letters to the Red Cross and wrote letters to the State Department, U.S. Embassy, the Haitian embassy in Washington, and even our state Senators and Governor, Mike Johann.

I got the following response from Mike Johann's' department:

Thank you for writing to my office to express your views and concerns, and I will send you a reply. It is an honor and a privilege to represent the people of Nebraska in the United States Senate. Feel free to contact my office and visit my website to send me your ideas.

Every day we set up a conference call with my siblings and kids so that all of us could call and learn from each other about whatever news we may have. Although some of us did not understand the conference's purpose, we all got the hang of it later.

We got a phone call to Haiti, obtained proper names and dates of birth for all the kids, and passed that information on in the letters we wrote. On January 16th, I wrote the following letter to the state department:

I am an American citizen in Nebraska, and I have my mother and sister in Haiti; I would like to return them to the US ASAP. My mother, Mary Rose Elizabeth Phillip, and sister Natasha Phillip and her children are also in Port-au-Prince. I want someone to see me with proper instructions on doing this. I am willing to travel to the Dominican Republic to get this done ASAP. I am also on the phone with other agents.

Thank you for your message. I got this response from the state department. Please confirm whether your mother and sister are American citizens or Legal Permanent Residents (e.g., have a green card). Also, please provide their passport numbers and dates of birth.

If they are American Citizens: Evacuation flights depart the International Airport in Port-au-Prince. U.S. citizens wishing to leave Haiti should proceed to the airport during the early hours as safely as possible. They are encouraged to carry their passport and identification, if available. They should bring as much food, water, and supplies - including any medication they usually take – as they can. There are limitations to facilities at the airport, and some seats are nonexistent. If they are LPRs traveling alone, they should contact the American Embassy.

We worked previously on helping my mother immigrate to the U.S. for medical reasons, so I gathered all her immigration papers together, hoping to help get her out of Haiti. Unfortunately, we knew the crisis was massive, and thousands of people undoubtedly made those duplicate contacts. Thus, it was no surprise that no one returned to us for several days.

When we finally got a return call from the governor's and the senator's office, they told us there was nothing they could do. We also received a call from the State Department, but they repeatedly said that they were only taking care of American Citizens at that point. We understood, but we were devastated.

I continued searching for a way to get to Haiti. Before the earthquake incident, I listened to NPR and heard an interview with the Omaha Medical School's new Vice-Chancellor. His name was Dr. Ruben Pamies. I noticed they were asking him lots of questions about Haiti. The broadcast grabbed my attention. Later, the interviewer revealed that the interviewing person was born and raised in Haiti. I researched further and discovered some of my other friends, like Doctor Jean Claude Desmangles and Doctor Alphonse Fouche, had already made his acquaintance.

Upon further inquiries, Dr. Jean-Claude and Dr. Alphonse have arranged for us to get together at my house. On January 17th, 2011, five days after the quake struck, we had a great opportunity. My wife found out that the Vice Chancellor for Academic Affairs, Dean of Graduate Studies, and Professor of Internal Medicine at the University of Nebraska, Dr. Rubens Pamies, was putting together a team for Haiti. From then on, Dr. Pamies and I developed somewhat of a friendship due to our connection to our beloved country of Haiti.

I called his house and talked to his wife, Michelle.

On January 18th, I sent the following letter to Dr. Pamies:

> Dr. Pamies,
>
> I am sorry I did not contact you sooner. I am so glad I had the chance to talk to your wife, and she explained very clearly that you are going to visit Haiti on Saturday. No commercial airlines are available, and I have been going out of my mind since Haiti's earthquake. It is a great miracle that my 79-year-old mother survived this. She is already a sick woman, and she is partially blind. They had to rescue her from the rubble; fortunately, she escaped with

minimum injuries. I am not so sure about my sister. She may have some broken bones. Thankfully, they have a cell phone, and we can communicate with her. They have been sleeping on the street since the earthquake.

My mother has legal residency in the United States; however, she has misplaced her documents and has not returned to the country in a long time. After speaking with your wife, I learned that they only accept physicians. I heard that they are running low on translators down there. Most of the Nebraska physicians I know are not Haitians.

I am willing to volunteer as a translator if they would allow me. I have sent several letters to Dave Heinemann and Mike Johann about this. I am sure if I arm myself with financial support papers, I may be able to get them here once over there. My wife is a nurse; she now works for the Red Cross. She also has been sending emails to the Red Cross. We sent some money to someone who traveled through the Dominican Republic. It has been a few days; the money has not gotten to them yet. They would use the money to pay for transportation to Cazale, a small town north of Port-au-Prince. My mother cannot continue to sleep on the street; I am afraid I will lose her if that continues.

I desperately need your help!

At first, they told me that I could not go because they were only taking doctors. Then, after offering my services as a translator (I speak fluent Creole French and have a good understanding of the Spanish language), On January 18th, I received an email confirming that I could go with the group as a translator since there was a significant need. The email read as follows:

Call my administrator Margaret at xxx-xxx-xxx and tell her I asked if you could go as a translator. You will need to give her some information to get clearance from the State Dept. I can't promise anything but let's try; I am heading to Philly tomorrow. I will check in later. Take care.

Rubens

Chapter 53

Trip Preparation

I now had two days to prepare for my trip, which was stressful! I used a Sprint-compatible HTC Google phone. I knew I couldn't use the phone once I got to Haiti, even though I had paid an additional $7 to make international phone calls. Sprint's tower collapsed following the earthquake, and they have not made any repairs yet.

GSM, a digital standard initially made available for purchase in 1991, was the most widely used mobile phone transmission technology worldwide. The Global System for Mobile Communications, an essential part of making and receiving calls, was used by GSM phones, claims Wise Geek. So, my wife and I headed to the Verizon Store, where they informed us about a GSM phone we could rent for the trip after answering several probing questions.

With the traditional "one channel per call" phones, the GSM standard employed TDMA (Time-Division Multiple Access) digital technologies, enabling three separate voice calls on the same "channel" as opposed to one ring.

Although a GSM phone offers more security than older technology, it requires the same transmission spaces. This type of convenient communication was made possible by digital compression. The inclusion of encryptions in GSM was also a bonus. As of 2022, according to Android Authority, GSM and CDMA networks were on the verge of becoming obsolete, given that 4G LTE and 5G were the current standards. Several US network providers, including AT&T, T-Mobile, and Verizon, are retiring their 2G and 3G networks, which rely on GSM and CDMA technologies.

We informed the Verizon salesperson that we would think about purchasing one of these phones even though we had no idea how simple it was to obtain a phone with a card in Haiti. They told us that until we used the phone and activated it, there would be no price. It can cost up to $2.80 every minute, though.

We visited a separate Sprint location where they gave us a different account of the tower's existence: They informed us that GSM phones would function on the Sprint network.

We decided to use the Sprint phone. It would be an "added line" in place of my present phone; we wouldn't need to rent it separately.

When we returned, we would purchase, utilize, and return it. If we bought the phone, the salesperson would also "incentivize" a 27% reduction in our monthly payments. My monthly expenses will be slightly less after all deductions than I had paid. What if I can't find a way to plug my phone in while I'm over there? I wondered suddenly.

I was introduced to the Solio charger by the dealer. Their website claims the Solio charger had technologies to maximize solar energy. It takes a Solio battery 8 to 10 hours to charge in direct sunshine. A fully charged Solio battery would provide up to 14 hours of additional time for your iPhone.

I bought the charger because it was on sale for $59. I emailed everyone as soon as I got to our house, telling them they could contact me on another phone while I was in Haiti.

I got a list from the trip coordinator. Gloves, a water purifier, a radio, a lamp that didn't require batteries, a camping bed, and fine clothes were also on the list of things we had to carry. It additionally had plenty of high-protein snack bars and t-shirts because the weather would be warmer than it was in Nebraska.

They advised me to take an anti-malarial drug and a cholera vaccine. I also have severe blood pressure problems, so I often take 15 medicines daily to be healthy. I thus updated my blood pressure medication and endeavored to acquire any additional personal or medical supplies I could require.

I was always searching desperately for items to acquire and bring with me that would benefit my family. Unfortunately, I didn't have much money to accomplish such a goal. I got permission from the University of Nebraska Medical Center to travel to Haiti via plane. Still, I had to pay for my flight from Omaha, Nebraska, to Fort Lauderdale, Florida.

To prepare for the trip, I left work early that day. The University of Nebraska Medical Center had planned a phone conference for 5:00 on a Friday afternoon the night before leaving. We went to the Omaha Wal-Mart at 132nd and Center to get some supplies to bring. We carefully browsed the sports goods section, attempting to select items that would be most useful on an island that had recently been devastated by a huge disaster.

I kept an eye on the time so that I wouldn't miss the conference. I had to listen to the speaker on my phone while a group of physicians worked out the specifics of the trip, so I knew I wanted to be somewhere quiet. We all had inquiries that needed answers.

Pediatric Endocrinologist Dr. Jean-Claude Desmangles, FAAP (Fellow of the American Academy of Pediatrics). He was a good buddy from Haiti who worked at Children's Hospital and Medical Center in Omaha. We called each other often to find out all we needed about the trip. He gave me some health advice about possible tetanus and malaria measures I should take. We made light of the products I had bought and the retailer I had done so (so he could avoid the store!) I was going to purchase everything in the store; he continued insisting.

When 5:00 suddenly arrived, I dashed to my vehicle in the Wal-Mart parking lot. Outside, it was a little chilly and rainy. Dr. Ruben J. Pamies, the trip's organizer and leader of the newly acquired expedition, had supplied me with the conference number and password through email, so I immediately shut the door and entered them.

The administrator requested that I identify myself as soon as she heard the beep signaling someone had joined the conference line. To explain why I was traveling to Haiti with the group, I quickly shared my tale while holding back tears. I carefully stated that this trip meant a lot to me since I could act as a translator because I'm not a doctor and had personal concerns that needed attention.

I could piece together the following facts during the last few days: my sister had a broken arm, my blind mother had been sleeping in the street, and some other family members had been hurt or were missing.

The remaining members of the crew began to show up one by one. The host welcomed everyone and presented Dr. Rubens when everyone arrived.

Suddenly, amidst her introduction, the phone rang in a booming voice. To our great confusion, the guy first introduced himself as someone who works with the State Department and the military. He then changed the subject to solar power and the needed materials in Haiti. The conference planner listens to him speak for at least five minutes before realizing that she is simply talking with an ungrounded solar energy marketer looking to close a deal. Dr. Pamies tried to convince the salesperson to hang up, but he kept doing so. That someone could be that disrespectful stunned everyone.

Dr. Pamies carried on with the meeting when we finally got him off the phone. We immediately realized that there was some uncertainty around our travel. First, we realized we needed to pack a few blank checks to cover the cost of the trip from Fort Lauderdale to Port-au-Prince. Second, we discovered that the plane we were chartering could only carry a certain amount of weight; we didn't want to take the possibility of overloading it, so we could only bring 70 pounds of baggage and personal belongings.

I had two brothers in Lincoln, Nebraska, who had taken considerable measures to set up a care package for my mother and sister, so hearing about this was not good news for me. Additionally, I had a box that my sister-in-law had put together. I had to get up the courage to tell them I couldn't send their bags to Haiti. Already I was dreading such conversations.

Nearly 70 pounds of only the stuff I needed for the trip were in my luggage, which weighed almost that amount. I didn't want to rely on finding suitable laundromats; therefore, I required a lot of T-shirts, underwear, and socks. Since I would be on the streets a lot, I got a ton of protein bars, a radio, and flashlight that didn't require batteries, a camping bed, some medicine for my mother and the kids, and my computer. Some friends had encouraged me to bring my laptop. We even spent money on a scale to make sure my luggage didn't weigh more than the permitted 70 pounds.

After the meeting, I returned to the store and discovered that our purchased items were more than $400. I tried hard to produce some things, but I realized I needed almost every one of the cart items.

I decided to forgo driving from Omaha to Syracuse that evening since my flight to Fort Lauderdale would depart early on Saturday morning. The weather would not have been ideal, and it could have taken me too long to get home.

Instead, I looked for the cheapest hotel near the airport using the HTC phone. We chose the Super 8 in the end. I took the shuttle to Epley Airport the next day. We sobbed together and hugged each other as I passed the security check. I refer to my daughter Hannah as courageous and sensitive since she and her fiancé traveled through the night from Tulsa, Oklahoma, to see me off at the airport.

Chapter 54

St Louis

The initial flight looked brief, and we stopped in St. Louis. We stood there waiting for the following aircraft with Dr. Pamies, his wife Michelle, and Dr. Odugbesan Oluyemisi, an anesthesiologist from Nebraska Medical Center (we nicknamed her Dr. Yemi). While Dr. Pamies was still working to arrange our travel to Port-au-Prince, we snapped photographs, visited the airport shops, and purchased some breakfast items. Everything was in transition. One second it appeared that our plane would arrive; the next, it did not. We took time to get more acquainted with each other. While sad, we still had a mission

One of the subjects discussed was the outrageous statement made by Pat Robertson on national TV: the Haitian people had made a pact with the devil to achieve their freedom from slavery. We did not know what to think about it. We were unsure whether Mr. Robertson suggested that the Haitian people have stayed in slavery or something else. As far as I can recall, I have always believed in God. I faithfully attend church and pray regularly, and I know millions of Haitians do the same. Listening to Mr. Robertson make such a statement felt like someone had just rubbed salt into our freshly wounded bodies. As if we were not hurting enough, we needed to worry more. All we could say was thanks, Mr. Robertson!

Before boarding the plane From St Louis to Fort Lauderdale, all four received a phone call simultaneously. The phone call was from the airline, which we thought was strange. We looked at each other with such amazement there was no need to utter a word. A recorded message told us our plane was changing the departure gate. We all hastily grabbed our luggage and ran to the newly assigned location.

When we arrived there, the attendant who stood behind the airline counter kept asking passengers to take a different flight free of charge voluntarily. It looked like the aircraft would be too jam-packed, she explained. The catch was that the other plane would first go to Chicago before routing us to our destination. Of course, we all declined. I had a million things on my mind. Something that I needed to do once I arrived in Florida. We quietly sat down and waited. When it became time to get on board, everyone got in line according to their seat number grouping.

First-Class travelers went first, then women with children. Finally, my group number came up, and I proceeded to the door, gave my boarding pass to the ticket agent, who swapped its bar code through the computer, and handed it back to me. After we were all on board, I did not realize how beautiful the plane's interior was. There were heart stencils and valentine's ribbon-like patterns all over the walls. Elderlies occupied nearly every chair.

It still did not register appropriately in my brain what was going on. Suddenly a message came over the intercom: "How many of you are members of our cruise?" Almost everyone lifted their hands except for us. The announcer kept talking; A few minutes later, she broadcasted with almost a whining voice: "It is someone's birthday..." She asked who else had birthdays that day; two kids also proclaimed it was their birthday. Suddenly, everyone was singing happy birthday. I did not know what to think, except it was bizarre. Ten minutes had passed; it was time for liftoff. One of the flight attendants stood in the aisles and went through the customary procedure of safety instructions in case of an emergency landing; a few minutes later, we were in the air.

The festive ambiance got heated up. The happy stewardess picked up the microphone again, and everyone clapped their hands. She began to sing some outlandish songs; apparently, the song was familiar to most passengers because most of them joined her singing. After the unexpected jubilee, she shouted, how many of you have been married for at least one year? Most passengers raised their hands. How many of you have been married for five years? Some dropped their hands. She repeated the questions several times while increasing the number of married years. Each time the quantity of raised hands dwindled slightly. The age qualification was 50, 55, and 60 until only one couple married for 65 years kept their hands lifted. Finally, she proclaimed them the winner and handed them a gift. I said to myself, Thank God it is over. I spoke too soon. She returned and said: Is there a couple among us who just got married? Of course, there was one who had committed the sacred act the night before. They as well received a gift.

Chapter 55

Fort Lauderdale

I took the shuttle to the Hilton Hotel. I wanted to stay with my brother, who lived in Fort Lauderdale. But unfortunately, I could not, and I learned that we all needed to stay together because we did not know when we would leave for Port-au-Prince.

So far, we knew we had to divide the group in two: one group will leave first, and the next group the next day or possibly later. The initial plan was a 5:00 PM Sunday departure for the first team and midnight Monday for the second unit. The night before, we had a meeting scheduled for 7:00 PM to review the plans.

I called my brother Estephan and told him where I was. He said he would be right there. So, I went ahead and checked in. When my brother came, he took Michelle (Dr. Pamies' wife) and me to the local Target store. I purchased some clothing items for mom and a disc for the Sony camera I borrowed from my sister-in-law.

As soon as we returned, it was time to start the meeting. At least one other than the group participants should know what is happening. At first, I asked my brother to rest in my room, and then I figured, 'why not invite him to the meeting?'

He took the elevator and joined us in the conference room on the second floor. I was staying in room 370 that night. I introduced him to the rest of the group, and the meeting started.

We learned that plans had changed. The first group was going to leave on Sunday at 3:00 AM, and the second team, which I was part of, will move on Monday at 3:00 AM. However, they told us to stay together because they could call us at any time for a meeting, and things could change.

That night, three Haitian Doctors, Dr. Jean Claude Desmangles, Dr. Gilbert Desmangles, Dr. Alphonse Fouche, and another Haitian Friend, Daniel Alexis, joined my room. They needed to use my computer to chat and catch up on emails. We took pictures and went to town in Daniel's car for supper. Daniel had a lot of stories to tell us because he went to Haiti the day after the earthquake; he went through the Dominican Republic. When he arrived in Port-au-Prince, they had not lifted all the bodies from the streets. He told us about the woman he saw whose lower part was outside while her upper leg was hanging somewhere else.

We returned to my room; we returned to the lobby and sat in the bar until 2:00 in the morning, chatting about different subjects.

The next day, it was Sunday, January 24th, 2010; I slept in the Hilton Hotel until I heard a knock at my door. The same group of friends had been there the night before. They wanted to use my computer more, and I let them in. At about noon, I looked at my phone and realized I had received several phone calls from Dr. Pamies. He was looking for me. He wanted to know when my brother would come and pick me up. He tried to determine whether we could go into town together to pick up some things. I informed him that my brother would not come until after work at 4:00 PM.

At 4:00, my brother Estephan came and got me and took me to a Haitian restaurant in Miami. We picked up some familiar food: goat meat, rice, and other goodies. When we arrived at his house, it was closer to 5:00 PM. He set up the table and offered me some starfruit I had never had.

Averrhoa Carambola came from Averrhoa Carambola, a tree native to Indonesia, India, and Sri Lanka. (According to Wikipedia, Carambola is also called starfruit. The tree and its fruit are favorites throughout Southeast Asia, the South Pacific, and East Asia. In addition, one can find these trees throughout the tropics, such as in Colombia, Trinidad, Guyana, Dominican Republic, Brazil, and, in the United States, South Florida, and Hawaii.)

I took a knife and sliced it – it does look like a cut star! I asked Estephan how to eat this; he said he washed, sliced, and ate it. So, I went to the sink, cleaned it, and took a bite. It was delicious. I ate about ¼ of it and proceeded to eat what we had purchased at the restaurant.

He offered to make me a cocktail, but I declined. While we were together, he dealt with his new wife, Lozanne. Lozanne is a Haitian physician my brother met a few months back while on a trip to see my sick mother. They fell in love and got married right away on the island.

My brother had sent her some money to travel to get picked up in Port-au-Prince. But, with all the chaos, she was trying to pick it up in the Dominican Republic. She traveled from Port-au-Prince through the Dominican Republic to arrive in Miami to join my brother; through little I could hear, they tried to hash out some wire transfer misunderstanding through the Western Union.

After several phone calls between Western Union and his wife, he had to leave me alone in his house to go and resolve the issue. While he was gone, I started getting phone calls from several people at the hotel: the group was looking for me. I had no way to get back to the hotel, and I had no idea how to give them directions to come and pick me up. I panicked quickly, so I called my brother and explained the situation. He came back and took me to the hotel.

When I arrived at the hotel, I discovered we would have another meeting immediately. Someone donated a plane – they had contacted several people, including John Travolta, to secure an airplane, and NASCAR was the group to come through. We learned they had booked our flight at that meeting, and we did not have to pay the $252 check.

I returned to my room and quickly created a group website. I registered the name HaitiRebuilders.com and uploaded some pictures.

We met in the lobby at 7:00 PM that night at the restaurant. Dr. Pamies advised us to meet in the lobby at about 2:45 am. I brought my laptop, talked about the site, and took pictures.

The group came up again to my room; our friend Alexis was there this time. Alexis had gone home and asked his wife to cook fantastic Haitian food for us. So, we ate it in our room, which was incredibly delicious.

After everyone had left, it was already after 11:00 PM, close to midnight. I took a shower and attempted to sleep, knowing I only had two hours to catch some sleep. I called downstairs and registered for a wake-up call at 2:00 AM.

I left the TV on for some background noise. The next thing I knew, it was 2:00 AM. I took another quick shower, brushed my teeth, put my bag together, and headed downstairs.

When I got downstairs, most of the group was already waiting for me. I went and signed out. They gave us some prepackaged breakfast. Now I needed to decide on my heavy coat that I knew I would not use in Haiti. I had the hotel store my jacket, and they gave me a claim ticket.

We all headed outside, and two buses were waiting for us outside. The drivers loaded our luggage, and we all boarded the buses.

I had no idea how far away we were going. When I came to Miami two nights before, the airport was like 5 minutes from the Hotel, and I did not know that

Fort Pierce was 107 miles away. As soon as we started to drive, everyone else fell asleep, and I was too anxious to close my eyes.

We drove for what seemed like a long time. Then, it started to rain somewhat. One of the nurses sat next to me and asked me to move to the left so she could lie down and sleep.

Chapter 56

Fort Pierce

We arrived at Fort Pierce closer to 5:00 AM. I did not know what to expect.

According to Wikipedia, "St. Lucie County International Airport Fort Pierce is a public airport located three miles (5 km) northwest of the central business district of Fort Pierce, a city in St. Lucie County, Florida, United States. St. Lucie was the owner of the Board of County Commissioners.

The airport sees frequent use by various aviation flight schools in South Florida, including three based at the airport, for general aviation flight training traffic. The airport also hosts a Federal Inspection Station (FIS) administered by the United States Customs & Border Patrol, making it a frequent stop for private aircraft coming in and out of the Bahama Islands.

Day Jet provided an on-demand jet air taxi service from this airport before it suspended operation in September 2008.

The airport's building history was from 1921 when The Commercial Club of Fort Pierce built an airport. Nine years later, the county purchased 1,600 acres of land that eventually became the current airport; however, the community dedicated the first commercial airport in 1935 near U.S. Route 1 and Edwards Road. The local American Legion building now stands on U.S. Route 1 for an airline that never got off the ground.

The current airport was initially named Fort Pierce Airport. It was leased during World War II by the U.S. Navy as an auxiliary field for pilots and flight crews from Naval Air Station Vero Beach, Naval Air Station Melbourne, and Naval Air Station Fort Lauderdale for conducting daytime and nighttime field carrier landing practice (FCLP) before landing on actual aircraft carriers. In addition, scout aircraft, dive bombers, and torpedo attack bombers utilized the military's runways to accommodate naval aviation training requirements better. In 1947, the Navy disestablished operations, and the U.S. Government conveyed the airport back to the county to include two newly constructed runways without charging for the improvements.

Curtis King, who became the first full-time director in 1967, played an instrumental role in developing the county's airport for 31 years. With little financial capital in county government to operate and maintain a modern airport, the facility languished for the next ten years, becoming overgrown with vegetation and subject to frequent grazing by cattle from nearby farms and ranches. Then, during the 1960s and 1970s, significant improvements occurred to rebuild the new airport terminal, modern hangars, airfield lighting, navigational aids, and fuel facilities.

The airport continued to evolve as a general aviation facility, even though they have decommissioned two of four runways. One such former track became the Airport West Commerce Park site; they have lengthened and improved the road 9/27.

I searched for something to tell me I was at an airport. We got off the buses next to what seemed to be a warehouse. Suddenly, I heard a sizeable vertical rolling door open; a gentleman wearing a life orange jacket and carrying a bullhorn came out. He welcomed us and immediately instructed us on where to put our luggage.

He showed us two wooden pallets. He told us to drop items we wanted to check onto the pallets and keep things we tried to carry with us.

The rain stopped for a moment. Some of us wanted to use the restroom. People at the airport told us there was only one bathroom, and just two could go inside simultaneously. One would wait outside the door while the other went in to use the restroom. Once we see someone come out, two more can go in. This activity continued for a while. Then, other missionary buses started to arrive.

The gentleman gave them the exact instructions. The rain started again; they told us to stay closer to the building not to get wet. They took our passports to verify whether we were on the list.

A forklift came out and took the palettes on which we had our luggage. They took them inside to weigh them. They called us one by one as we entered the premises. The total weight of our checked-in baggage was precisely 700lb, and we had about 200lb left for our carry-on luggage. Remember, we had 13 people in our group, and each should not have more than 70 lbs. So, the maximum weight we could carry was 70 times 13, around 910lb. Everyone clapped because we did not exceed our weight limits.

The 'warehouse' was a big steel building with a white sign and blue background that said, 'Missionary Flights Int'l "Standing in the Gap" for Missions.' Far away outside, I could see at least 4 or 5 airplanes on the ground. On the left, I could see a DC1; on the right, I could see thousands of boxes with labels marked with items destined to go to a different part of Haiti. One of them said, "For the people of Carrefour, Haiti, from North Carolina;" another one said, "Towels/Blankets."

They aligned several white plastic chairs facing the wall. There was also a long metal railing behind the fence.

I could see the entrance to the infamous bathroom and another closed blue door. Between the two doors, there was a large electrical panel.

They lined up three or four long tables. On top of the food tables, they had cereals, Juice, milk, coffee, doughnuts, and bagels; underneath the table, you could see all the open boxes of Cereals and where to use them. Meanwhile, forklifts were lifting palettes full of cargo and moving them all over. Some were in the process of reorganizing them, while others were loading them into small planes.

Several soldiers in camouflage uniforms started to arrive. The atmosphere was partly festive and sad at the same time. Everyone there was headed to Haiti to help.

Chapter 57

Port-au-Prince: 2nd Airport

Our stop in the Bahamas was short; we were not there for vacation or pleasure. I snapped a few pictures after the plane was on the ground, waited for a few minutes, and refueled; we started the upward motion that would surely take us to Haiti.

To my left, I saw nothing but the ocean for a while. We approached the outskirts of Haiti; on my right, I saw mountains. The plane seemed to be going extremely slow. Finally, the captain announced we would start our final descent to Port-au-Prince. I could hear the landing gear cranked into motion; it was a good sign, I said to myself, and finally, the last bumps that indicated the tires had touched the ground. The captain welcomed us to Haiti and told us about our stay on the plane.

The flight attendants opened the left door and extended the mobile stairs to get off the plane. A gentleman came on board to explain the procedures. We looked around; there were Americans all over. Other than the trees, the building, and the temperature, one would think you were not in Haiti.

He welcomed us to Haiti and started to explain immigration rules since the earthquake. "We are operating out of this small airport because someone has reserved the bigger airport for big cargo planes and the military," he said. They asked us for our passports, and each of us gave them to him. Then, he ordered us to stay on the plane until he returned.

We waited for half an hour; another gentleman came on board and instructed us to get off the plane. Some of us refused. He assured us the processes took longer than expected; he needed to unload the aircraft, but we would be OK. We got off the plane and formed a line as we headed toward the building on the ground. In front of us, there were several Americans lined up behind a rope line.

It appears they were getting ready to leave the island. We waved at each other and proceeded to get inside the building. The ambiance was almost the same as I remembered it 30 years ago when we got inside. Several young men in uniform and badges were eager to help you with your luggage; some looked worn and anxious to make a few bucks. The first thing they do is grab your bags and start to head outside.

We told them we could not go outside because security had not returned our passports. I would call one of these panhandles to assign himself as my help. The driver told me his name and immediately told me about his story and what happened during the earthquake. I gave him a five-dollar American bill, and he looked at me like someone who had just given Bill Gates a dime. He said, "What do you think I could do with that?"

I said, "Wait a minute. You have not done anything yet for me." I pulled my phone out of my pocket and noticed no signal. I asked the rest of the group, "Does anybody have a phone signal?" They all said no. My 'personal helper' told me that I could use his phone. Max was my sister's new husband or boyfriend. I was not sure at the time; I had never met him. Nevertheless, I called Max, informed him that I had arrived, and asked him to come to the airport where I was.

Meanwhile, we are still waiting for our passports. I needed to go to the restroom. Since the earthquake, no functioning lights or running water have been functioning. No one took the necessary measure to provide some indoor facilities; they probably had something outside, but we were unaware. I located the restroom sign and started to head toward it. I struggled to find the light switch; oops, no light. I went back outside and asked for more info. My guide told me; I would have to use the bathroom just as it is.

When I returned, one of the nurses remarked she had traveled to a worse region of the globe than this. She assured me, though, that she would be fine; after all, she had gone there and successfully returned. "You are the bravest person I know," I exclaimed as we waited for our passports.

Meanwhile, I saw a crowd 10 feet away from me, surrounding a lady holding some papers in her left hand. I tried to get closer to see who she was. Then, It was Congresswoman Maxine Waters, I realized. Maxine Waters has served in the United States House of Representatives since 1991, representing California's 35th congressional district. She lives in the Hancock Park neighborhood of Los Angeles, about six miles west of downtown. She is a senior member of the African American women in the United States Congress. Everyone naturally wanted to chat with her.

Rubens introduced us to the congresswoman, we took some pictures, and she talked to us. I explained to her my inability to get papers from Senator Ben Nelson, Mike Johann, and the State Department so I could take away my mother and my sister from Haiti. We chatted for a while; she received my name, phone number, and email address and assured me that she would consider it when she returned to Washington. Unfortunately, I have not heard from her as of this writing yet.

After a few more minutes had passed (they seemed like hours), the man with the passports returned, explaining that he had to drive to the main airport to have our passports stamped before returning. Then, he called each of our names and handed our American Passports back to us. We all were grateful we did not lose our Passports; we expressed our gratitude to God.

We assembled our suitcases when Rubens told us that Medishare, a hospital within walking distance from the airport, expected the doctors to begin working immediately. Rubens asked me if my driver was outside; I told him yes. Meanwhile, Max (the driver) and one of my cousins were outside waiting. Everyone took their luggage out and took off to the hospital, leaving their bags behind, except for Dr. Alphonse Fouche and me, who stayed back.

Since 7 in the morning, they have been tired and hungry. I remembered that my wife had bought tons of protein bars. I reached into one of my suitcases, unzipped the bag, and passed out the protein to friends who came to see me. They were happy to have it; the food calmed them down slightly.

A UN bus came by and wanted to take the entire pile of the doctors' luggage. We did not get instructions about what would happen, so Dr. Fouche and I refused to let them take the bags. We went inside to find out where all the other doctors had gone. I went further, past the yard where all the planes were, and continued west toward the Medishare hospital. We could not find them, and we still had to wait.

An hour later, Dr. Vladimir and Dr. Pamies came out. Dr. Pamies indicated that he was going to his sister's house. I asked him if he had a way to get there; he assured me he did.

Chapter 58

Earthquake Destructions

Haiti's most notable structures have designs from French Renaissance architecture. The earthquake devastated essential sites such as the National Palace, the Palace of the Justice system, and Ministries.

The National Palace came about as a result of great competition. The people of Haiti erected it in 1918, with Mr. George Baussan winning the architectural battle. It was a two-story, all-white edifice with three gazebo-like buildings or pavilions. I've never been inside, but from what I've heard, seeing the palace always has been a wonderful experience for any lucky visitor.

When we visit a solid historical landmark, knowing it has been there for centuries, we can't help but hope it will be there for another.

The structure that shelters our belongings does not have a voice to alert us of its danger. Unless there is a need for restoration or repair, the roof that shelters us from the weather doesn't get daily admiration from us. We do not appreciate someone we care about until they are immobile in a casket.

It is incomprehensible that people act as if they have the right to possess anything or be openly ungrateful to someone who constantly helps them. This type of ungratefulness is "taking things for granted." you also believe it is your God-given right to enjoy that privilege perpetually, which is not the case.

Earthquakes happen, as we all know. It's in the news, and the Bible mentions it in Matthew 24:7. "Country will rise against nation, and the kingdom will rise against kingdom. Famines and earthquakes will occur in numerous locations ". Unfortunately, there is no way to prepare for an earthquake effectively. In our thoughts, "many locations" constantly allude to someone else's backyard. Nobody believes it could happen to them.

Haiti has seen multiple storms as well as political upheaval. Based on local culture and wealth, societies offer shelter and suitable community infrastructure. Building regulations did not exist as they should have, and many people died.

We are seeing these people's life and prized goods shattered by the ferocity of a significant earthquake. The uproar that follows is something that no one wants to endure.

Living in Nebraska, I've seen the devastation caused by unexpected tornadoes on television. After watching such havoc on the news, I usually attempt to comfort myself that it is all a dream. I persuade myself that the reality I live in is still working usually. I can resume my normal activities without hesitation.

I've seen movies that show the destruction of buildings. It had occurred in a few houses or an entire neighborhood.

However, I had never witnessed such calamity in a place where so many people live so close. Overpopulated areas are a daily thing in Port-au-Prince.

Television reporters from the United States and other areas of the world have combed through the ruins of Port-au-Prince and reported on their findings. It was just another narrative to them; most of them had been in combat zones before. They can maintain their gaze fixed on the camera and express the pain to the best of their abilities. They can return home, be influenced to some extent since they are human, and regulate the impact on their mind. It was different for me.

I have a genuine connection to Port-au-Prince and its inhabitants, and I could tell you stories about some of the demolished structures. People I hadn't seen in over thirty years may be among the deceased.

I understood as I strolled through the streets of Port-au-Prince following the earthquake that this would be an event I would never forget. I discovered that material goods might vanish in the blink of an eye. We feel our worth is as flimsy as a spider web and as transient as a puff of chilly air in a Nebraska winter.

Every street had debris mounds strewn over the walkways. My nose was overwhelmed with the unmistakable whiffs of yet-to-be-removed dead people, making me question my sanity for being there.

I wrestled with inconceivable thoughts mixed with pity, but self-determination triumphed as I remembered all the locations I had yet to explore.

Each structure has its own story to tell. "I used to go to church here; look at it, there's nothing there," I remarked, motioning for my driver to pull over so I could take a snapshot.

"Look at this one; it used to be a grocery shop," my sister added. We could see the rear entry of the building next to it, which had an SUV half buried in the garage.

"This school was where my brother Benjamin used to teach. I understand that not all buried remains have been retrieved, "I motioned to someone. I looked to my left, right, then farther ahead at the mountain. There was not a single structure that was unaffected.

The people in charge of dismantling the impacted buildings marked them with orange or red demolition markings; others already had teams working hard to clear debris. Unfortunately, none of the donations provided by worldwide communities have yet arrived where they are most needed.

We could see small groups of locals with wheelbarrows, shovels, and picks. Some organized a queue to transport manageable concrete pieces to the sidewalk. Occasionally, they would come across a body and scream out loud, abandoning the premise until they could safely bring it to the sidewalk for eventual retrieval.

These giant rocks and fractured cement blocks with embedded metal will require extra attention and heavy machinery to complete the task correctly. They will need excavators, tractors, and construction equipment to retrieve unseen bodies. They would have first to remove twisted metal rebars, but how would they utilize them? So I told myself quietly.

I tried not to weep as I walked past each structure, recalling how I recalled them thirty or forty years ago. I couldn't take it any longer when I reached the building where I grew up. The overwhelming despair that had filled my spirit struck me twice. First, I was unaware I was harboring intense feelings. While my immediate family had survived the calamity, many others had not. I felt terrible and needed to cry for people who the tragedy had impacted. Second, I was unclear about what feelings I should think on behalf of my father. He worked diligently to provide a comfortable home for his family and seeing mother nature in such distress

Our family was rapidly expanding in 1965. My parents and five children shared a one-room flat with other family members. A curtain separated their bed from the corner table.

The girls slept in one corner at night while the boys slept in the other. When the sun went down, we shared the little table to complete our homework; during scheduled blackouts, we used our gas lamps to see. Every night, Dad would tell us stories about how he would construct a house large enough to accommodate our room one day. We trusted him because dad was a guy of conviction who always kept his promises. As the oldest son, I had the privilege of sharing complete details about the family business.

I recall dad telling my mother and me about the acreage he had bought from his landlord. "Son, I just spoke with Mr. Athea, who owns some land outside of town and has agreed to let me buy it from him. The nicest aspect about the arrangement is that I can pay him in installments."

My father knew Athea's family as one of the most prosperous. They owned the land on which my father operated his car repair company. My father's social standing was quite different from theirs. We used to go to his house in Petion-Ville, an upper-class town. We generally went there to pay the shop's lease; it was always a joy for me to go there.

The residence was cared for by a butler, servants, and gardeners. They lived in a two-story house with mosaic floors, a beautiful yard, and a television. It was unusual to see a place with a television in 1965.

"What a wonderful father! When are we going to be able to view it?" I was ecstatic in response. "How about we take a taxi there on Sunday, and I'll have you meet the neighbors?" Is it necessary to wait until Sunday? Why can't we go tomorrow since it's only Monday?" I confronted him.

"We have some paperwork to sign, which I won't be able to accomplish until Friday," he stated. Every day that week, I asked him how many days we could see our land. Finally, I marched confidently into my playground, telling my pals everything about it.

People began to regard us differently. We suddenly became a family who possessed something that distinguished us. We hailed a cab when Sunday finally arrived. I recall Dad telling me about specific structures in the taxis. "This is General Hospital, where you were born.

Do you notice all the shops across the street? There, they mainly sell shoes. The Silvio Cator stadium is on your left." Silvio Cator was born in Cavaillon, Haiti, and the people of Port-au-Prince elected him Mayor in 1946. Mr. Cator was a Trivoli Athletic Club and Haitian Racing Club member who excelled in soccer. In 1924, he competed in the Olympics in Paris.

At the 1928 Summer Olympics in Amsterdam, he earned a silver medal in the long jump. His record has remained unbroken as of this writing, at least for the Haitians. The Grand Cemeteries — the Great Cemetery — were many acres in the heart of Port-au-Prince that housed the deceased of our country's most notable and influential families.

The Grand Cemeteries is a one-of-a-kind landmark with magnificent mausoleums and other gravesites. Despite being enclosed by an eight-foot cement block fence, It was not difficult to see some of its residents' buildings since they were taller than the wall.

Today, the cemetery has more living people than dead following the earthquake. Thousands of people moved in out of necessity, frequently evicting the already deceased with gasoline and matches. The massive mausoleums resisted the shock better than many substandard communities.

There is also a Christian church and ceremonial voodoo stands, meeting the spiritual demands of the people who resided in The Grand Cemeteries.

I noticed the peak and a little hill as soon as we passed the cemetery.

As we passed the cemetery, I saw a colossal hill they called "Mount Nelio-Morn Nelio." "Are we going to live on the mountain?" I inquired innocently.

"We will not get to the mountain; our land is just a few blocks after climbing the hill," said my dad. I looked through the cab's window and watched people's day-to-day activities. I had never been in a neighborhood like this at ten years old.

Some of the structures struck me as bizarre. "There's a major hospital about a block away from our land," he instructed the driver to approach it closer so that I could see it. I saw it; it was larger than life—a vast white edifice with gates and many stories. I learned later they do tuberculosis treatment there. The taxi driver halted for a few moments to have a closer look. Then he turned around. He had to honk many times as pedestrians were everywhere.

When we arrived at the location where our address was, neighbors looked as my father paid the driver as we exited the cab.

"I don't see any empty land, Dad," I remarked puzzledly. I kept asking questions. "You'll see it soon enough," My dad smiled back. "It's hidden behind this home." We entered a corridor and passed two buildings. Very few houses face the street in Haiti. "Where are we going to sleep tonight? I asked sarcastically.

As we explored the area, one of our neighbors approached us and introduced himself. My name is "DuNor." I quietly snorted a little bit. "What kind of name is that?" My dad shushed me as I smiled and attempted to move away from them.

After a few moments, two more interested neighbors approached my father. "Go ahead and assist by gripping the tape measure's end and measuring as far as you can. Keep your grip firm!" One of the men instructed me. I grabbed the tape and almost stumbled on one of the pebbles. "Be cautious!" he exclaimed. "Nearly a hundred feet," he estimated.

As a youngster, they did not aggressively include me in their adult conversation. Instead, as I recall, they spoke about how many rooms they could put on that small plot of land and how big the rooms needed to be.

My father responded, "I can only afford two rooms at first, so we can move in right away."

Two spaces! Already, we had twice as much as before! "When can we start moving, Dad? By when?" I echoed with evident excitement.

"Son, calm down. The engineers you assisted with the tape are the ones who will build our house. We won't be able to move in for a few months, but we'll stop every weekend to see how things are going ". He gave his explanation while feeling accomplished.

My father and I went to see our future house every weekend. I would return with fabricated tales about how tall and steep the mountain was. The incredible antics I pulled with my younger brother Estephan around this time are what I recall most clearly. He had never been there and was just six years old. I would make fun of him by saying, "Estephan, they had to use a rope to get us up there." I said, "I imagine I won't drop you a rope so you can climb if you don't share your food with meat with me." The poor boy would always approve and give me the meat off his plate.

As time passed, The builders completed the two rooms, and we relocated to our new home. They returned later and added a kitchen, a bathroom outside, and a shower inside. Since there were no doors in any of the houses, we utilized bed sheets as door curtains. We barely used half of the land for the two bedrooms we had. For as long as I can remember, the other half had six to eight mounds of gravel in a corner. I recall having fun with the neighborhood kids during games.

We had a four-foot high, twenty-five-foot long cement block wall as a barrier between the neighbors to the south and us. With the help of two pieces of wood and a white sheet fastened in the center to create a theatrical screen, one of my best friends and I would pretend to be filmmakers. We would carve various figures with rifles, including buildings, horses, cows, and cowboys. We would thread a string around two wood bobbins in the center of each piece of wood. We would put the string figures and light lamps behind the screen when it grew dark at night.

As we moved the dolls back and forth by spinning the bobbins clockwise and counterclockwise, we added our voices and music and created our movies, complete with plots. Making this entertainment for our friends and relatives became second nature to us. We soon began to charge other youngsters who wanted to watch one coin. Our "movies" sometimes lasted an hour since laughter frequently broke them apart.

Three more rooms, a porch, and the house's completion were all done by my father. He also used cement for the roof's construction. My favorite place to do nearly anything became the top. I went up there to study, play my guitar, and listen to shortwave radio to learn English. For the house, my dad engaged a craftsman to create custom doors from natural wood. They finished the living room's floors with mosaic tiles.

My parents welcomed Jayden and Gabriel into the family nine years later; Jayden was born in 1971, and Gabriel was born in 1973. It was a significant deal for our family since it was rare for a family to wait so long before getting pregnant again. By the time my last brother came around, I had reached the age of sixteen. The doctor mistakenly believed my mother to be my wife since I was old enough to drive her to the hospital while she was in delivery.

In 1978, when my youngest brother was just five years old, I left Haiti to study in Nebraska. My dad built a second floor with a contemporary shower and flushing toilet while I was away, replacing the initial half of the house's corrugated tin roof with a cement roof. There were six rooms up above.

My father's passing in January 2001 marked the end of a stable environment.

I went to my old house after the earthquake when I got here. I was observing the debris from where I was standing. I tried to talk to several neighbors, but they didn't know me because I hadn't been there in so long. Eventually, two kids showed me where I could go and save my mother. A little gap where the upper floor gave way, and the bottom level crumbled. Should I mourn or give God the glory for rescuing my mother? I did neither because I didn't know what I could do. I could not talk to anyone since no one knew who I was. My sister and mother lived in Cabaret since the building was no longer there. All I could do was take a few shots and then drive away.

Chapter 59

Trip to Family Members

I returned to my chauffeur and his buddies and requested that they transport me to my mother's location. He was driving a Camionette at the time. In Haiti, they usually convert a regular pickup truck called a Camionette to accommodate people. They are usually quite ornate, with religious inscriptions in front and on either side of the vehicle.

Passengers board by walking on an integrated rear step. Inside, two long benches face each other. I sat in the driver's seat. Max slid my two red and black duffel bags between his legs, and one of my cousins sat in the rear. I apologized to the driver for Max having to take so long. Whatever he said, the passengers in the back could hear us since an open window allowed the driver to interact with them.

I hadn't been in Haiti for a long time, so I peered outside. It was a dusty and heavy cast of sunlight, with only a few clouds in the sky. When I reached my location, my dust-covered hair made me look like I had aged a few years.

I requested my cousin to get me a dust mask to protect my breathing from the dust. I knew I had one in one of my duffel bags, but I couldn't find it immediately. She struggled to locate it. I put it on as fast as possible to prevent breathing the outside dust. They suggested that I roll up my window.

The roadway appeared to be congested. Since the earthquake, some residents of Port-au-Prince have relocated to the countryside. In comparison, Syracuse,

Nebraska, has a population of roughly 1852 people. So here I am in a metropolis with a population of about 9.7 million people, according to World Bank/ Development Indicators. Some may argue that this is unfair because you must compare countries and cities. But keep in mind that Haiti is just around 10,000 square miles, whereas Nebraska is nearly 70,000 square miles on its own. As a result, you can physically fit seven countries the size of Haiti within Nebraska lands.

I quickly observed the distinction between the trees on the island. Compared to the eastern Dominican Republic side of Hispaniola, they have used most of Haiti's trees for charcoals and building construction without planting new ones. As a result, Haiti has become a highly deforested country, with life-threatening floods and mudslides regularly occurring due to massive soil erosion caused by a lack of trees. Concerns like these, of course, become less critical during crises like an earthquake.

It was on a Monday afternoon when I arrived in the capital of Port-au-Prince, but we were soon heading away, and I would not witness any of the destruction caused by the quake that day. Instead, we drove east into the countryside. I could see an open road ahead of me, mountains to my right, and the ocean to my left.

When I looked to the right, everyone in the car requested I take a picture of the first wrecked structure I could capture.

I could smell the ocean, but that freshness faded when we drove through the 'Valley of the Dead.' Finally, around 10 miles off the main road, someone said, "This is the location." "Where exactly is that?" I replied.

"This is the mass grave site; they daily take bodies in truckloads there." However, when the world saw this on CNN, several Haitians were startled; this was not the first time they had witnessed a mass burial in action. People have seen truckloads of unidentified remains dumped in the region throughout the years, either owing to political upheavals or abandonment at local morgues. The only difference was that we simultaneously talked about tens of thousands of dead. Nothing may be more sobering than a reminder of the insignificance of our earthly life.

We were going at approximately 40 to 50 miles per hour, and the terrible stench began to fade as we drove away, to be replaced by the natural purity of the ocean.

"How far is Cazale or Cabaret from here?" I inquired of the driver.

"We still have more than an hour to go," he remarked. When I was ten years old, I had gone to this Cabaret previously, and I do not recall it being so far away. As a result, we continued driving and encountered horses, cows, and goats wandering wild all over the roadway.

I shouted whenever I saw a herd of horses, cows, or goats. When one of the animals came too close to our vehicles, I jokingly called: "Get out of the way, dobby," like in Crocodile Dundee's movie. Sometimes we had to come to a complete stop and honk our horn several times before they moved away, confused.

I occasionally observed two, three, or even four individuals riding the same motorcycle. I once witnessed the motorcycle's rear passenger carrying a load of shredded metal from wrecked structures. A little motorbike with two persons on it would drive past, and the one in the rear would be carrying blocks from damaged houses.

The camionette came to a halt and turned right. "Are we there yet?" I inquired.

The driver made a shaky motion with his head. We started down the dirt road toward our destination. There were houses lined up on both sides of the road. Children were playing on the street while adults sat on their porches. Cazale/ Cabaret, once known as Duvalier Ville, is stunning. Latitude: 18° 44' 04" N Longitude: 72° 22' 26" W; Statistics estimated the population to be about 10,000.

However, this figure may be higher because a census had occurred before the earthquake.

I spent the remainder of the afternoon getting reacquainted with my mother and other family members. Since the last time I saw any of them, some crucial members had grown up and had grown-up children. Suddenly, the conversation turned into the details of how mother survived when her house collapsed on top of her. Who got injured or not? I learned then my sister Natasha had a broken wrist. Not knowing how chaotic the next day would be, I promised her I had just arrived with a group of physicians and, hopefully, I would arrange for one of the doctors to examine her wrist.

As I continued to speak with each of them, I found they were all uninformed of the earthquake's magnitude. I tried to convey what I witnessed traveling from the airport to Cabaret. My phone's battery was running low. I couldn't show anything to them. A picture, as they say, is worth a thousand words.

My mother summoned someone with a trustworthy battery to charge phones, usually for a price. That individual charged up my phone for free since he was intrigued about what was on it. After a few hours, the whole neighborhood gathered around me to view footage and photos of the devastation I had witnessed. There was a sign of sadness and anguish across the group. Fear made them more unstable than ever, as they recognized the earthquake had removed the majority of the reasons for them to visit Port-au-Prince.

Chapter 60

Community Hospital – Day 1

The group I flew from Nebraska with urged me to meet them the next day at the hospital where physicians treated earthquake victims. After breakfast and a long trek back to Port-au-Prince, my sister Natasha, a chauffeur, and I headed toward the hospital. We had to stop three times to ask for directions; we finally arrived at the facility around 1:00 p.m.

It was a private facility. The earthquake did not cause considerable damage to that building; they transformed it into a typical treatment facility. It was a new setting for me. My primary goal was to help Natasha fix her wrist and complete my assignment with my traveling companion.

A mass of folks split into different areas in front of the facility appeared discombobulated. People were trying to avoid the sun's scorching punishment. I could see automobiles parked on the right side of the road, on the sidewalk, and beneath the trees. A long line had formed in front of the hospital's entrance. I told my sister and the others to stay there while I looked into what was happening.

I made my way through the mob to the entrance attendant. A tall American security gentleman stood in the center of the entrance, flanked by two American troops. They requested I present valid identification. He specifically asked to verify that I was part of the University of Nebraska delegation. I handed him my driver's license. As soon as I spoke and explained who I was. He responded: "Good enough for me." He acquired a name tag and fastened it to my chest. I signaled my sister to come with me.

I went inside first to ensure the doctors I was traveling with were there. I discovered three of them. Dr. Odugbesan Oluyemisi, an anesthesiologist who gave me a tour and explained the triage concept, was the first. The term "triage" is from the French verb "trier" (Tree-ay), which signifies separation. They separated individuals based on the severity of their diseases because there were no specialized rooms where they could execute the necessary procedures.

A group of people argued 25 feet from the entrance as security decided where to send them. One individual worked as a translator for US security troops. Communication did not appear to flow as it should have due to the apparent misunderstanding.

Patients were lying on hospital gurneys and stretchers at a drugstore across the aisle, near one of the building's sky-view segments, within the first sky-view area. On the right was a chamber that housed drugs and acted as a backup pharmacy. This site has to have been beautiful before the calamity. With the flower arrangements still in bloom, it was clear how wonderfully they adorned the hospital - but there were a lot of patients about now.

Many physicians got sacked, sweaty, and overwhelmed by the number of patients that required their attention.

My immediate remark was that no organizational structure existed. Doctors used sheets of notebook paper and scotch tape to attach them to each door. When the doctors had finished seeing a patient, they would admit them to a room, and any available nurses would write the patient's name and status on the notebook paper.

Most physicians would do the same, taking notes on their papers and providing observations and directions for the following doctors or caretakers. Some Doctors occasionally forget or do not have time to write their names next to a request. It wasn't clear how to proceed to the next step because technicians, nurses, and translators like myself had to figure out who had ordered the surgery before the doctor could do it.

They admitted patients in the same haphazard manner. They tried their hardest to be fair and sympathetic to everyone, but their efforts were haphazard. A patient would receive priority if someone could plead their case with whoever was "in charge" at the moment (and in that place). Occasionally, one of the doctors would notice a patient who had been there for an extended period and would take the time to expedite their treatment.

They had built an immediate Mobile Army Surgical Hospital or MASH unit (similar to the TV program) in one region. Several victims were screaming in anguish, while others lay tolerantly on the floor, hoping that aid would arrive soon.

I had a brief conversation with some of the doctors and informed them that I would be working with them as a translator as soon as they repaired my sister's wrist. They told me to bring her in. I went back outside slowly through the crowd, repeatedly saying excuse me. I dashed out, signaling to security that I'd be back.

When I arrived at the parking lot, my sister Natasha and the driver were not where I had left them. I searched about eagerly till I spotted them again. I escorted her and her husband inside. We located an empty bed in a room where three people were already waiting for us with the assistance of one of the American Nurses.

Two patients were on stretchers on the floor. One was lying on a table they had converted into a hospital bed. The first patient got a left leg external orthopedic fixation device (EOFD). (An EOFD is a metal bar (or several) inserted through the skin directly into the bone, usually on either side of a severe break. It sits outside the limb, functioning as a "backup bone," keeping the bones on each side of the gap completely aligned so that the rip heals appropriately.

The screws pass through any muscle in the way and bite deeply enough into the bone to hold the light, an overly complicated metal bar in place.) Her leg swelled, and some tissue around the metal screws; That poor girl was in agonizing pain. She had to have been there the day before. The physicians debated whether to retry the operation or finish the amputation.

Meanwhile, one hospital staff mended the corner bed, and I urged my sister to use it while locating one of the physicians.

I noticed two other American physicians conversing in the aisle. They were debating how to do a transtibial amputation properly. The first stated: "You must first determine the diameter of the limb where the tibia will be severed. Remember to prevent amputation of the distal 1/3 to 14% of the tibia ". "There is no muscle tissue there, barely covered with some padding," the first doctor stated. One doctor glanced at the other, puzzled, and demanded an explanation.

I recall studying about the tibia and fibula while in a summer pre-med program. I was intrigued, but that didn't stop me from asking one of them to take a look at my sister. So I got closer and listened more. "We must allow the tibia to break at the distal end... Yeah, yes, yes! Correct posterior flap, correct posterior flap! The surgery should take place around the soleus muscles and the Achilles tendon. We will leave roughly 6 to 8 inches of space below the knee if the client has to use prosthetic feet ".

A female doctor returned to my sister's room. The doctor examined her and advised her to have an x-ray immediately.

I arrived at the Radiology department after traveling through two corridors. I requested instructions for the x-ray room. I passed through a swinging door with the label "Authorized Personnel Only" written in black magic marker on paper and taped shut. I could travel practically anywhere in the hospital with the one-of-a-kind tag on my chest that security had given me.

I saw that the nursing stations either had too many attendants or none. Instead, there were army gurneys or stretchers containing patients along the corridor; some had casts on their legs, while others were waiting for x-rays. When I turned back, one of the physicians had followed me with my sister. We had a lengthy debate over who should go next. Finally, one person who arrived with a family member asserted that they should go first because they had been waiting since the previous night. I addressed the person at the entrance and told him I wanted an x-ray done.

When the X-Ray technician exited the room, he observed the physicians and myself discussing. He got my sister in and conducted the x-ray as quickly as I explained how vital it was to have my sister repaired so that I could help others. After waiting outside the x-ray chamber, someone returned with a large brown package. He addressed us by name and presented the x-ray to the doctor.

The doctor instantly examined the x-ray film by bringing it to a bright light. He discovered several near the window. He began to describe what he had seen to us. "It appears to be a distal radius fracture." "It seems more like an intra-articular fracture," said the second doctor. The fracture had penetrated the joint. There had been much too much time between the time it had shattered and that day. The bone's location was utterly out of place. A cast could work, but the hand would still appear malformed even after the damage healed. She would very certainly always be able to move her fingers. Surgery would be a far better option.

"If it were my sister, I'd have the surgery," the first doctor added. "The procedure should take no more than twenty minutes, and she will be able to go home immediately after recovery. Let me return to the surgery room and see if we can fit her in", he finished as he walked away.

It was coming later in the afternoon. My sister returned to her designated room. As soon as I returned to the hallway to see if I could speed up the procedure, one of the physicians summoned me to duty. He was working just across the room from my sister. He had a thirteen-year-old girl behind rocks with smashed legs. One of the legs was severely lacerated and excruciatingly swollen. She couldn't put her foot down to walk without screaming.

The doctor had undergone an intricate procedure of customizing an adult metal underarm crutch so she could walk. Her mother was seated next to her on the floor, but neither knew what the doctor was saying. It was time to do what I had volunteered by coming here.

The doctor initially adjusted the pads and, using my understanding, indicated that they should be positioned against the ribs beneath the armpits while keeping the grasp. Most crutches include a push-button height adjustment to suit people of various sizes. The doctor attempted the lowest spot, but the crutch legs remained too lengthy. He removed the rubber tip and all the screws required to disassemble the gadget.

He opened a toolbox and took out a rough hand saw. He began to cut. He was sweating as he attempted to cut through the crutch leg. He eventually managed to reassemble the crutch. We had to try three or four times until we got the right height. I helped the small girl stand up as she sat on the chair, still weeping. The doctor helped her place the crutches beneath her arms. I tried to keep her from falling back down into the chair by holding her. We gave her instructions on how to use the leg devices through translation.

"Move both crutches forward first, then the good leg, and finally the damaged portion. Try to maintain good posture by standing as straight as possible. Check your destination by looking up", we informed the young lady. After numerous trials, we gave her mother instructions and asked for another case.

I went by short to check on my sister. Finally, the doctor caring for her returned to inform us that he had gotten her on the schedule.

At the same time, I had engaged in another conflict with my chauffeur. He was unhappy since he had been with us, therefore, locked up by our service. He had spent the entire day with us and was growing frustrated. He would repeatedly send someone to inform me that if we did not leave by four p.m., he would raise the amount agreed in our agreement. "We should get you out of here by five," he promised.

"Please realize that my sister will be having surgery soon. We will take care of you for your time. Just wait a little bit longer, and we can bring you some food if you need it, "I implored him. I made some phone calls to the United States. I told the rest of the family what was going on. My sister communicated with her daughter in New York, who set up a conference call with other family members. I explained to them what was going on. They required a translator in the hospital's open area after I got off the phone.

I watched in horror as a young lady lying down on a stretcher had four toes wholly crushed when I got there. The doctors tried to mend her wounds, but her toes were beyond bruised; they were entirely dark blue. The doctors told her (through my translation) that they would have to amputate them to prevent them from getting further infected. Nevertheless, she was grimly brave when she heard the news and thanked me for my service.

When I returned to my sister, she was getting restless, also. The doctors had told her she could not eat, but she had not eaten all day. Further, she was getting quite nervous about sleeping inside a building. Many Haitian people, my sister included, had developed a genuine phobia of being inside – the continuous aftershocks kept damaging more buildings, and often, structures that looked strong would collapse for no reason anyone could tell. When the roof becomes a deadly threat, sleeping inside becomes something that can frighten anyone.

The doctors came back and said they had to hurry up to save the life of a lady with a crushed pelvis. Since it was a life-threatening situation because of the extensive bleeding, they needed to use a metal physical device to keep the pelvic area in place while taking care of any other injuries she may have had. They feared she would not make it through the day if they did not take care of her immediately. Her health was precarious, and time was a significant factor.

Due to that and several other emergency patients, they bumped my sister's schedule to ten PM. When I explained this to her, she went ballistic – of course. She insisted that she would instead come back the next day. Unfortunately, the driver wanted to return to Cabaret, and my sister could not sleep inside a building, no matter how stable it seemed. I negotiated with the doctor to come back the next day. We went back to Cabaret that night, each of us utterly exhausted.

Even though I merely completed my day's to-do list, I accomplished a lot. We received an x-ray for my sister, we took photographs of Port-au-Prince, and lastly, I had the opportunity to assist some American physicians in treating some injured patients. However, I was still uneasy since my sister was in agony, and I blamed myself. She was barely surviving on Ibuprofen and whatever else the doctor gave her. I hoped there was something else I could do.

The journey back to Cabaret was nothing short of thrills. The vehicle's front right axle required overhauls, and the tire oscillated oddly and unevenly. We had to stop many times because the entire car was severely shaking. On one occasion, we heard a loud and terrifying noise coming from below the truck and used the brakes to bring it to a halt. The driver and his companion left our car to check the sounds. They spent some time determining that it was a pebble striking the oil pan at the proper angle. We returned to the car and drove to our destination at 6:30 p.m.

Since I had left early that morning, I did not have the chance to chat with many people. However, when we returned, I took the time to do so. I talked to my mother and my sister's kid, and they provided me with more details about the earthquake, and I recorded some of their stories on my camera.

Chapter 61

Community Hospital – Day 2

We returned to the same Community hospital the next day. I was displeased with the way things had played out the day before. I was hoping they'd send a new crop of doctors. And my chances of fixing my problems may improve. Some people who came with me on the trip worked at various hospitals. I knew several of my medical buddies worked at Port-au-Prince's Hospital since they rotated them around to optimize their expertise in dealing with diverse situations. I hoped in my heart that I would run across one of them in my current place.

Nevertheless, I was irritated because I had access to over twenty doctors, but none could help me. My anger was palpable; how could I not even get a cast on my sister's fractured wrist?

When we got to the gate, we walked through security again like the day before. The people at the gate knew me at this point and let me through without incident. People clashed as they strolled along the hospital aisles, engrossed in the millions of thoughts racing through their heads. We ran along different corridors, saying "excuse me" as I peered around for a familiar face.

Suddenly, one of the doctors who had visited me the day before appeared. He approached me directly and had a lovely discussion.

"I had your sister scheduled. Unfortunately, another life-threatening situation arose, and we had to reschedule her appointment. I'm very sorry, Robert", one of the physicians replied, sweating while walking

"I don't want to spend the entire day here again and go home without repairing her wrist," I told the doctor severely. "Do you want to wait till evening again?" I inquired of Natasha. "I've had enough ibuprofen...I want to leave things alone. "She expressed her remorse.

"If it were my sister, I would take her to the United States. Why don't you describe the problem to the American Embassy? "Said one of the doctors behind me. "I didn't notice you! I responded. "With a doctor's letter, the X-ray negatives, and the other immigration paperwork, you could have a fighting chance at the embassy." He added, "Let's talk about it, "I said with eagerness.

"I'd want to go to the embassy, but I doubt the papers I have will persuade the American embassy to let my sister leave the country," I explained. "You have nothing to lose; how about we prepare a doctor's note for you to take?" one of the doctors offered. "That would be incredible!" I almost screamed with joy.

"Come with me, and we'll find a counter or a desk somewhere." He said as we rushed to find a suitable area to write the hopeful memo. Finally, we were assigned a room near the surgery room. We rummaged through paperwork strewn across the receptionist's desk for official paper and a fountain pen. Unfortunately, they were dry and useless. We discovered loads of paperwork stowed in cabinets but no fountain pen. Suddenly, we came upon some on the ground.

Finally, the doctor found one, along with a medical prescription pad. "What are your sister's whole name and birth date?" he queried, sweat dripping from his brow, threatening to destroy the letter he was diligently composing.

I stared at him as if someone had asked me a problematic oral exam question, and I couldn't recall the answer. "I should know this," I said timidly.

"Just a second, I want to double-check... Natasha!" As I turned around to seek my sister, I shouted. She was standing hardly two feet away from me. She was still in pain with a makeshift towel wrapped around her wrist. "Again, what is your birth date? Too many thoughts in my head...." As I asked the doctor additional questions, she laughed and gave me the answer. The doctor gave me two unique letters to go to the embassy; one would assist my mother in coming to the United States, and the other would help my sister.

According to the notes: "Natasha is Mrs. Phillip's sole caregiver because Mrs. Phillip is half blind. Natasha was injured in the earthquake and required urgent medical attention in the United States. Mrs. Phillip and Natasha have families in the United States that can care for them. Any assistance from immigration officials in obtaining a visa would be greatly appreciated." The doctor signed it with a flourish and smiled as he handed it to me.

I glowed with evident gratitude as I shook his hand to thank him.

One of the most challenging things to convey to an outsider is that my sister was still living in Haiti after the earthquake. Even our family's closest relatives sometimes find it challenging to comprehend. Yet, here we were, eight kids spread across the globe from Nebraska to Paris, and she was the only one who had never left Haiti.

I am somewhat always guilty about the whole situation. On the one hand, Natasha had opportunities on multiple occasions to secure a Visa from various documents we have prepared and sent to her. Unfortunately, a successful conversation with the consulate prevented her from getting a Visa, as we all did. On the other hand, I deliberately add the term "somewhat" since the degree of guilt that pierces my heart every time I watch my younger sister dealing with the hardships that are endemic to living in Haiti): Natasha was a married woman with numerous children while most of us were dealing with Visa issues. When the time came to petition for her immigration, we reasoned (rightly or wrongly, I'm still not sure) that having one family member available to care for my parents and the house my father constructed was critical.

When one of our parents died, Natasha had a daughter in the States. We mistakenly thought if the daughter filed for her instead of the brothers, it would take no more than six months to complete the process.

I then contacted Cabaret and my wife, and my other siblings in the United States to inform them of my plan to get a Visa for Natasha. I told my sister and the three gentlemen accompanying me of my decisions.

Finally, I shakily urged everyone I spoke with on the phone to pray, explaining that what I needed to do would be incredibly difficult to complete in the limited time I had.

Chapter 62

General Hospital – Day 3

To heal my sister's wrist, I still had one more day. As I already indicated, the doctors that traveled with me had tasks that required them to visit several hospitals. The last location I needed to look for a solution for Natasha was Haiti General Hospital. Even though I had some documents to work with to obtain my sister a Visa, I thought acquiring an orthopedic cast for her wrist was more critical.

I contacted the driver, who assisted us at the community hospital for the first two days. He suggested I use his Jeep as he had other appointments scheduled for that day.

He handed me the key to his car after I paid him a little cash. This time it was just Natasha and me. I got to Port-au-Prince's Hospital around eleven o'clock in the morning. There was terrible traffic on our way there. When we arrived at the hospital entrance, we had been driving for two hours.

Since I had to drive, I was already starting to get exhausted.

We wandered around the hospital yard for eternity after security had let us inside the gate. We were hoping to run into someone we knew.

As a result of the earthquake, they have repurposed all portions of the hospital. There were covered tents in the space where parking used to be. I heard someone shouting my name out of nowhere. Doctor Pamies was standing there as I turned around. Three other doctors accompanied him. These medical professionals came from a distinctly east coast delegation. I told him about all the problems I experienced at the community hospital after he introduced me to them. He apologized for not giving me instructions to come to General Hospital on the first day. "It doesn't matter anymore," I interrupted him. "The main thing for me now is to get a cast. How soon can you help with that?" "Let's do that now, he responded." Suddenly I felt a sense of relief that I had never felt before. Turning to my left, I noticed a big smile on my sister's face.

He led me on a short hike to a far-off tent, where he introduced me to several of his buddies. There were various stations in the tent where technicians and medical professionals attended to patients needing orthopedic casts.

Outside, a queue of individuals was awaiting their turn. Some experienced severe injuries, while others had a minor arm or leg fractures. Doctor Pamies explained my predicament the day before and begged them to move us ahead of everyone. Additionally, he revealed to them how long Natasha had been using Ibuprofen. One of the physicians replied, "You know, all these folks are earthquake victims, and they've all been in agony for a long time." Since you are in charge of all these places, I will take care of Natasha immediately.

I gave Doctor Pamies my sincere appreciation for his assistance. We departed the hospital and moved to the Embassy.

Chapter 63

Visa Quest for Natasha

It has never been a simple task to visit the American Embassy, especially when securing an appointment and a visa. When I arrived at the immigration facility, I observed that the procedure for entering was more restrictive even after I became a naturalized American citizen.

Following the earthquake, security, comprised of local officials and American soldiers, was even more visible at the entrance. As my chauffeur and I drew up to the gate, two guys signaled us to turn left, even though I made my desire to move forward apparent.

The street outside the Embassy was hot, dusty, and extremely loud, with construction vehicles honking automobiles and individuals begging for alms or assistance. The car in front of me made it. The passengers inside had an extended conversation with the foot troops. I halted in front of the gate, and one of the guards approached me. "You can't go inside right now," he snarled.

"I am an American citizen; I need to see the American consulate," I said, my voice matching his.

"You need to walk south ways, turn around, and enter the embassy from the west side," he roared like a rock band member. After a brief and useless dispute with the gunman, I turned my car south.

We found ourselves on a dirt road where most buildings were still under construction, and relatively few appeared to have been damaged by the earthquake. We continued south for a long time, unable to locate a way to turn west. Finally, we saw a short lane like the entry to someone's villa. It had an iron gate on both sides, yet it was open. We approached cautiously and found ourselves in a maze of houses — a development area where only the Twilight Zone theme music felt adequate to capture the ambiance.

We ended up on dead ends three times and couldn't get out. We came to a halt twice to ask for directions, and the last set of instructions we obtained from a pedestrian led us to an open marketplace. None of us wanted to confess that we had lost the path of where we should have been going, and it looked like we'd gone too far south, far away from the city where we were.

Finally, a half-completed roadway brought us back to town. It was already scorching when we reached the opposite side of the Embassy. There were a couple of metal barriers on each side of the street, and two local policemen sat beneath a tree in the subtle shade. They grabbed their firearms and marched toward our automobile as soon as they noticed us. "No one is permitted to enter; you must find another entry!" said one of the cops.

"I am an American Citizen; I want to go to the American Embassy," I exclaimed with an adamant voice.

"I don't care; you're not coming in!" He yelled back at me. In my life, I've learned that it's never a good idea to dispute with those who carry firearms.

I did a U-turn and saw some American troops directing traffic two blocks away from where they were. A pair of emaciated-looking, hungry youngsters approached, begging for food, but the Americans had nothing to offer them. I came to a halt and struck up a polite discussion with them. I introduced myself as a Nebraskan and thanked them for coming to aid in this calamity.

So, I reached out into my bag, found some high-protein bars, and handed them out. One of the soldiers said, "That's what we need to carry with us!"

After a few friendlier conversations, one asked me about my mission. I said, "I just attempted to get to the American Embassy, and the Haitians soldiers told me I could not." Finally, one of them hopped in my car and said: "Let's go!" Hope swelled in my chest – and gratitude.

The expression on the faces of those Haitian soldiers is something I will never forget. We just waved at them as we passed through the gate. After clearing the security area, the American soldiers got out of the car and said, "You are on your own now." I thanked him as he closed the door, and he turned and said: "See you safely back in the States, Robert." I thanked God for the soldier's generosity and turned to look at the Embassy grounds.

The embassy entry was on my left: two long rows of cement barriers created an alley with awnings in the middle, secured by metal poles driven into the obstacles. At the alley's entrance, two young American troops stood side by side. I was concerned about talking to any forces at this time, and I resolved to avoid them if possible. I felt like I'd walked into a State Fairgrounds without the rides — just people: a few merchants and thousands of onlookers.

I walked behind the tent along the barriers. The first twenty-five feet of the building lacked awnings, and two more troops sat on folding chairs beneath the covered space further back. I attempted to cross over after reaching the end, where I didn't believe there were troops. When one of the soldiers noticed me, he started running toward me with his gun as if he was about to engage in defensive action. I knew he'd have many questions, so I prepared myself. I stayed still and quiet as I awaited his arrival.

"What do you think you're doing?" he said, alarmed and intrigued.

"I am an American citizen; I urgently want a meeting with the American consulate," I explained carefully. While explaining to him who I was and why I was there, I battled to maintain a sincere grin. I mentioned that I had traveled from Nebraska with a medical team to assist with the earthquake relief effort. I devised an honest narrative to persuade him that he had no choice but to help me—the more truthful my tale, the less persuasive I felt I needed to be.

One of the troops described the kind of persons they were ready to process quickly: injured Americans and other categories announced by the State Department. Since the earthquake, they have been shifting priorities hourly and daily. However, they did not include the close relatives of injured American citizens on any list.

Suddenly, I could present myself as part of the group helping injured Americans needing transportation to Miami within the next twenty-four hours, or things would get ugly. There was some truth to that, but it didn't matter as I felt desperate and gradually began to add to my tale. I needed to spice things up or match some of the standards. I needed to start thinking differently, or I wouldn't get very far. The longer I talked, the brighter the empathy in the soldier's eyes got.

He rapidly led me through the troops' lines, instructing me to relate my narrative to each of the guards. I had narrated my story to four guards by the time I reached the end of the tent. Finally, the last guard unlocked the gate, and I entered the Embassy's front yard. I was all in! I maintained my account stable again, riding the enthralling and urgent streak.

One of the guards led me inside the building and directed me to a window with thick glass and a small aperture, like a ticket window at a movie theater. Three individuals sat behind the glass, behind the counter.

One lady spoke to the person in front of me and adjusted the table's microphone so she could hear him better. The gentleman was dressed formally in a Haitian army uniform and looked to possess a position of great importance in the Haitian military. He murmured a few things to the lady, and she exited the room. While I was waiting, he struck up a discussion with the soldier who was accompanying me. "My kid is in the American military," he proudly informed the soldier. "With which division is your kid serving?"

"I assume he resides in Kansas," said the Haitian cop. As they discussed their interests, the lady behind the plate glass window turned her attention to me and motioned that I might go in the yard, and I thanked the soldier and entered.

I walked out to the yard. Within a minute or two, a tall, dark gentleman approached me. He introduced himself, stating he was from New York and handled the process of weeding out persons so that only the most pressing situations would take up the consulate's valuable time. As I told the soldiers outside, I began to say to him my tale.

I quickly felt concerned since I couldn't read him and didn't know if he believed me. I began to reply as I did to the troops by bending the truth somewhat, but my conscience warned me that this was wrong. I voluntarily came to a halt in the middle and resolved to return to God's path: the truth. "Look, I need to be honest with you," I explained.

"I don't have any injured physicians that require rapid transportation to Miami. As a result, you don't need to send a helicopter to Cabaret.

Cabaret is a commune in the west part of Port-au-Prince. This little town was once known as Duvalierville, after François Duvalier. The name survived until Duvalier's successor, his son Jean-Claude Duvalier, left the country in 1986. In 2009, the commune had 62,063 people. Some of my relatives on my father's side reside in Cabaret.

My sister has been injured and is the sole caregiver for my 79-year-old mother, who is partially blind. She has a fractured wrist. I am genuinely a member of a Nebraska team assisting with medical aid. I have x-rays and paperwork from two physicians with me. I'm attempting to acquire paperwork to bring my wounded sister and blind mother to the United States on Friday. Can you assist me?" I poured out my emotions to him.

"As much as I would love to help you, the American Embassy has strict rules; we only process specific kinds of people on specific days. Today, we are processing orphaned children and injured American citizens only. I can get you through if your sister and mother are American citizens. Otherwise, nothing will get you to see the ambassador today." He carefully explained it to me.

The disappointment began crawling over my body as he talked and talked. Finally, his voice started to recede from my ears. I felt weak, worthless, and extremely thirsty at the exact moment. "You could have another alternative," he said. "You may take a gamble and travel to the Dominican Republic's boundaries. Perhaps someone will be sympathetic to your situation and allow you through."

I had no idea how long I had circled outside in the scorching heat. Finally, I peered ahead; there were at least two or three cases of ice water bottles heaped up by the gate. "Can I bring some water with me?" I begged frantically.

"You may take as much as you can carry." The gentleman spoke to me quietly as he looked around to ensure no one would object to his charity. Last time, I grabbed four or five water bottles and begged him. However, the more I talked, the clearer it became that his decision was definitive.

I went outside since they had just beaten me in a boxing contest. I dug deep into my soul for some reason to justify my failure. I searched around but couldn't find the driver. He needed to relocate the automobile a few streets away without telling me. Sweat was streaming off my brow as I departed the Embassy, despondent yet unsure of what to do next.

I crossed the street to get some shade from the scorching sun. A distressed lady was speaking Creole to me. She wanted to know whether I was successful, and she had a scenario where she needed to get in. The poor woman had no idea how to approach the American soldiers.

As much as I wanted to help Natasha or explain the issue, I was now more anxious about finding a ride back to Cabaret. I knew Max would not abandon me, but the heat made me worry about how long I could wait for him to locate me. I spent at least two hours at the Embassy.

I paced back and forth down the street for at least fifteen minutes before noticing him and my sister approaching. I expressed the refusal, and we prayed for the strength to drive back to Cabaret.

Chapter 64

Faith Tested

Regardless of your age, life may be incredibly challenging. Most of us have encountered situations that frighten and unnerve us. When bad things happen, and you feel powerless to stop them, life might challenge your faith. The most important thing is how you respond to these situations, so you do not lose control.

The birth of my first child, Rachel, and the subsequent diagnosis of SIDS (sudden infant death syndrome) is a beautiful illustration. Her mother and I had to spend a lot of restless nights with one eye open as the first year of life challenged our faith to the utmost.

We received a kid monitoring device for SID from the hospital. That was before expensive cell phones were available. It appeared to be standard medical equipment with cables fastened to the baby's body. While she slept day and night, we had her hooked up to the monitor. The monitor's job was to make sure she didn't cease breathing. Every time the alarm goes off, especially at night, I would jump. These restless nights left me with an emotional scar I'll never forget.

The alarms did go off frequently, but thankfully we mainly experienced false alarms brought on by frayed wiring. Regardless of whether it was a false alarm, we got out of bed since we did not want to take a chance.

Since we had four kids, we had to keep the monitor on all of them to make sure nothing terrible happened. Hannah, our second child, required it for her first 13 months. Michaela, our third kid, was observed for eight months before Celeste, another child, was monitored for six months. We made it through those years, and thank God nothing significant occurred.

Our first child, Rachel, began to have arm and leg numbness at the age of 20. Her physicians prescribed an MRI (Magnetic Resonance Imaging), a non-invasive diagnostic procedure that produces in-depth pictures of the body's soft tissues. They determined she had MS (multiple sclerosis). The doctors explained a person with MS, an incurable disease, may frequently feel tired, numb, tingly, weak, dizzy, and painful, have trouble walking, have cognitive problems, and experience vertigo and vision problems.

There is no set schedule for the progression of this disease; it worsens over time. Better than others, some people can handle it. She has been doing a terrific job following a program to strengthen her immune system, and everything is well. We are not sure how long.

Even while our religion promises us that we will overcome this, we constantly prepare for whatever comes next. Even though our kids are older, we understand that the emotional test is far from over.

Rachel was going through a divorce in the wake of the tragic earthquake in Haiti in 2010, and two of her kids started becoming sick. Rachel has moved to Yakama in Washington State. She needed help because her hubby at the time couldn't be there to watch the kids.

We relocated from Nebraska to Washington State after multiple phone conversations and flights to Washington. By being there, we eased Rachel and our grandchildren while working with very little savings.

It was not a pleasant surprise to learn that our first grandson had neuroblastoma at the age of 10 months. The tiny glands on the top region of the kidneys are where neuroblastoma first appears (adrenal glands).

It can develop in the bones, neck, pelvis, chest, and abdomen. The afflicted region may have a lump or compressed tissues.

The most impacted children are those under the age of five. Fatigue, appetite loss, and fever are a few signs of neuroblastoma.

Sam may have surgery and chemotherapy for this cancer to remove the tumor. We watched him closely for seven years.

The experts warned us that seven years would be crucial since cancer may come back. The seventh year has passed, and praise God. He is becoming more and more vital in the Lord.

Our second grandchild, Katherine, was born with a deformed kidney. She was born with a third kidney. Katherine had surgery to reimplant her ureters at the age of 18 months. She developed meningitis and had to stay in the hospital for a month.

Elizabeth, our third grandchild, suffered a nose-to-tail airway obstruction. Before she became one year old, she required nine operations, and medical professionals also found a hole in her heart.

In addition to her shaky marriage, my daughter Rachel was dealing with all of these issues. Because she had relocated to Washington State with her unreliable husband, she desperately needed assistance.

We were forced to sell everything we owned, including our retirement savings, and go to Washington so we could assist.

As Rachel's marriage fell apart, she returned to Nebraska with her children. God sent her a new friend in 2017. We pray for God to continue to bless her new husband, Sovida, and the kids, who have adapted to him quite well.

Chapter 65

Precious Memories that Last

Our year-end trips between July 1965 and September 1970 were extraordinary. Our grandma was just in her mid-to late-50s, so she was still youthful and active. But every year from when I was five years old until I was twelve, mom would fly from Gressier to Port-au-Prince to fetch me, my younger sister, and my brother up.

Small town Gressier is eight kilometers from Leogane. Gressier's population was at 75,000 in 2017. The approximate distance from Port-au-Prince is 12.5 miles. It is a little town with a 41.11 square mile area. It may be seen on a map in the southern region by the Gulf of La Gonâve. Gressier and the community of Carrefour share boundaries to the east. It is also near the Momance River and Leôgane city in the west. Its three principal rural neighborhoods are Morne à Chandelle, Petit Toucan, and Morne à Bateau.

Gressier's population was much lower in 1960. My mother, father, and four children made up a family of six. My father immediately gave my grandma enough cash to utilize for transportation and food for at least two weeks when she arrived at our home in Port-Au-Prince.

It was an adventure to get to Gressier from the city. I recall my grandma taking us to a bus stop in the middle of Port-au-main Prince's street. People were constantly on the road, yelling about the goods they were trying to sell.

A bus station was only one of the neighborhood's street corners that the locals had informally set aside for buses and Tap-Tap to pick up passengers.

One bench was on either side of the interior, primarily handmade. Tap-tap translates as "quick-quick." typically, the owner of these Tap-taps haphazardly embellishes and paints a pick-up truck with traditional sayings.

Each Tap-Tap, or camionette as some refer to it, had a representative. Within two blocks, an agent might move around and recruit potential travelers. The agent repeatedly yelled the bus's destination town's name as she made quick movements about the area. Each Tap-Tap had to adhere to predetermined itineraries, and it didn't leave the station until it was overflowing with people. A passenger may disembark at any time throughout the trip.

We would raise our hands to indicate that we had the proper agent as soon as the agent uttered Leogane three times. He would then hurry up, seize our luggage, and follow us. Sometimes a five-block merry-go-round is required until enough people fill the entire tap-tap.

The agent would simultaneously use one hand to hang onto the rail and another to wave down further people.

Years later, one of my favorite musicians, Rodrigue Milien, wrote a lovely song recalling this element of Haitian society. Every time I hear the music, that particular moment comes to me.

When we entered the car, we had trouble finding a comfy seat. There were almost ten persons seated on the five-person benches. Without exaggeration, individuals were sitting on top of one another. It wasn't easy to see the view well. Many travelers lacked a place to unwind. We sat down next to strangers. My sisters, brother, and I occasionally sat on Grandma.

They had hundreds of little baskets, bags, and luggage on the tap-tap. There have never been any limitations on how many people can fit in a car of such kind.

There were big horizontal stairs at the back entryway. Several customers and staff took hold of a little rail to secure themselves. They stayed still while the car accelerated to 20 to 30 mph, filling their lungs with road grime, car, and another carbon monoxide.

It would take approximately an hour or two from arriving at the station until we reached Gressier.

Our legs would hurt when we eventually arrived and exited the tap-tap, and we would have to walk for at least 15 or 30 minutes. After that, we would picnic there, eat our meal, and continue walking for another 15 minutes until we reached the first river. There were palm, coconut, mango trees, and several mangoes. The water was stunning and sparkling.

There were substantial boulders in the middle of the river that passersby had aligned to make the crossing easy to endure. Then, we would walk another 15 minutes to climb a mountainous area. That was the most challenging part of our journey to our grandparents.

To ensure no one was hurt when climbing these mountains, folks from the farms would meet us nearby. They arranged the baggage on the horses and donkeys that they brought. Typically, the ascent took 30 minutes, not because it was a lengthy, somewhat difficult route that required us to go slowly and halt sometimes.

After navigating the mountains, we came to a fundamental level route we had to travel. The ground was red clay soils, which anthropologists refer to as ultisol. These soils include calcareous minerals.

No more than two individuals may travel on the route at once. On either side, there were weeds and thorny plants. They will put their feet on yours if you are barefoot. To escape the prickly plants and potential snakes searching for sunshine, we had to walk in the middle of the road.

They would be picked up and thrown on the farms on either side of the road by passing individuals. People would have their farms, and we would have to climb a small mountain and descend a hill to get to my grandparents' house.

Rooftop dry palm trees. The houses had lath and white clay plaster for the walls. The clay was pure white and formed a permanent bond when mixed with water. These houses have a front porch, but there is no carpet, wood, or anything; it is flat earth for the floor. They were like beds from the 18th century because they had no nails. They had ropes and poles, and the mattresses were from banana trees. They try to put them together with strings and so forth, and they look like a bit of a bed, but it is a work of art; they are gorgeous.

There were four bedrooms in grandpa's house, and at that time, he was a person who had a little bit of money because he had a lot of land and farming and so forth. He had so much ground that he usually left one part of his Jam-close farm to the house. So, we had two avocado trees and a couple of coconut trees, and in one part of it, he had a lot of sugar cane, and the rest had corn.

Because we don't have winter, they would start planting corn in the middle of January and February. Those months are perfect for growing corn; In the middle of January, they get many friends and workers and plow the land by hand. They don't have machines, tractors, or anything; they do everything by hand. They would sickle the area and get all the weeds out of it, and the next day they would rake the land.

They could cultivate many acres, and it would take about a week or two weeks for 50 to 100 people to get this work done, and this was how they would plant their corn. When the corn is dry and ready to be harvested, they will invite many people in the neighborhood, 100 or 200 people, and they would come and pick the corn with their bare hands, put it in baskets, and then make packages with them. To do this, they took the corn, one ear at a time, and peeled it. Then they tied it down with the next ear until they had a pack, and at the end of the package, they took a rope and fastened the cable in there, then dug holes in a palm tree, one or two or three holes, and climbed up in the palm tree and let the corn hang there. The farmers do not use their crops; they have harvested the same year. They typically wait until the following year.

The only part they will use of the young corn is what they cook; they prepare it differently.

For breakfast, we used a cornmeal drink we called "Akasan." Our parents gave us a bowl of Akasan and fresh bread rolls with butter. At the time, this was the prevalent type of meal in Latin America and the Caribbean islands.

The preparation was simple: Mix corn flour with a cup of cold water. Add a simple dash of salt and anise. Let the water boil and later lower the temperature. Pour the Corn-water mixture into the boiling water. Add vanilla extract; add evaporated milk and a little grated lime rind. One would continually stir to prevent globs from forming in the corn concoction.

Some refrigerate the mixture if they like to eat their Akasan cold the next day. Cold or hot, you add some sugar or evaporated milk. Our parents advise that we remove the anise before serving. We ate Akasan the same way we ate cereal in the United States in the morning.

In the countryside, farmers followed different processes with corn. After harvesting corn, they dry the grain; my grandparents invite people over. Then, they put together wood barrels, take the ears of corn, hold them with one hand, and twist it until all the kernels fall into the baskets. The task takes days to complete because they don't have any automated way to achieve the mission.

When they finish with the corn, they must take it to someone with a grinder and grind the grain. Some in thin powder, some in medium, and some more granular. Haitians called the more granular part of the corn "Tien-Tien."

The history behind the Tien-Tien was a word the enslavers used to share the meal with the enslaved people. When you give somebody something, a French person would say "Tien," which means "Take this." During the slavery period, Haitians used this type of corn, and the French masters would say "Tien-Tien" to them, so, therefore, they called this type of ground corn "Tien-Tien."

As our summer vacation continued, we would get up early in the morning and go to our garden and camp close to the nearest river, sometimes, it would take hours to get there, and when we did get there, we would camp and eat watermelon or sugar cane. There was always enough food there; you didn't have to take any food for the camping trip; my grandparents had food everywhere on their farm. They had watermelons, different mangoes, and various types of sugar cane. We would go fishing. Usually, we used a basket for fishing. We constructed a pail, attached a rope to one hand, and dipped it into the river.

There were many rocks in the rivers; some children would take days to remove stones and create a big hole, a sink, so the fish and crabs would come into it. Then they would dip the 'basket in the water, and when they picked it up, they harvested different crabs and fish. We used to go hunting, also. We would take tire rubber and a piece of a tree branch that looked like a "y." We make slingshots to kill different birds. I remember most about our summer vacation when my mother went with us, and my parents came to see us.

I remember one incident with an enormous snake. My mother and her sisters were doing laundry in the river and everyone else in the area. The river was nearby, and the water was beautiful and so bright you could see rocks and fish several feet below. Different kinds of trees surrounded the river, mango, oak, etc.

One morning, my sister and I needed to take food to my mother by the river. Each time we encountered an obstacle on the road, we jumped over it. Then, as most kids do, we made a game out of it.

Sometimes it was just a tree branch, and other times it was just a rock. That morning, we saw something that resembled a part of the tree that may have fallen on the road.

We were about to jump over it when it suddenly moved. We looked around, and there was nobody close that we could see. My sister screamed as hard as she could, and I tried to console her and decided to make decisions on where to get help.

It was a giant snake about the size of the bottom of the most prominent tree. It was huge, regardless of whether the person looking at it was a child or an adult. As the snake slithered around to move away, two men working nearby came down to help us. These two men had machetes with them and voraciously killed the snake. Later, I heard they ate the snake, and others described its deliciousness.

We went on our way and took the food to our mother. After that, my grandparents started to like my mother and father again. They forgot about the past, even though my parents were not married.

You have probably heard the story about the zombie; yes, I learned about the zombie myself during our yearly three-month vacation. My intention in this book is not to reveal secrets but to explain what I witnessed. There was a rumor that everybody who lived in Port-Au-Prince had a lot of money, so my father took a chance, and when my mother came to visit us, he sent with her a lot of presents for grandpa and a lot of gifts for grandma.

The zombie situation was that people with financial means in the farm area often wanted people to work for them, but sometimes they did not want to pay for them. So, when there was an argument between two people, if one took another man's wife or somebody wanted to make his part of the farm produce more crops, they would pick a potion for these people. They make a drink out of pufferfish; there is a part of this poisonous fish.

They would have a ceremony, and they had different ways of giving this potion to the person. A tiny drop of that drink is so deadly that it can kill somebody, so they need to take precautions about how they give it to you. They can give it to you in your food or blow it on you. They have different ways of doing that, and the person would be clinically dead, but the person is conscious that the person would know what is going on. Still, his whole body becomes immobile, and although the person is aware of what is happening around him, he cannot do anything. I remember personally meeting a zombie man, and he told me how one of the nails got into his head, and he could not cry; he felt everything but could not move; he could not do anything.

Our grandparents' house was very close to a cemetery, and at night we would come out and sit down with grandpa, and he and grandma would tell us stories. Most of the time, we had a humor about these things. My mother almost killed my grandmother and grandfather because of a joke. My uncle wanted to play a trick on my mother, so he took a blanket, put it on his head, and went around the house. When my mother opened the door and saw something white in front of the house and said a zombie, she panicked well.

The next day somebody knocked on the door again, and she came out with a pan and opened the door, and started beating on my grandpa with the pan, and when they got inside, they were laughing about the whole thing. Every night when we could not see the moon, we had no electricity, but when it was a full moon, we would sit out and tell stories.

They used to tell us all kinds of stories about kings and queens, and it was beautiful, but every night, and with the cemetery so close, we would witness people walking by in a group. Someone told us: There they are! We saw people going in and out of the graveyard. Someone would continue with the explanation as part of the story. "You see, the way they do it after a person dies, whispering, they have about 24 hours to go and exhume the body. First, someone gives the targeted person a well-prepared potion to drink, and that person would then be under their control. When they get them out of the tomb, they would have white blankets and tie that person's hands behind his back. The zombie would be in front; the person directing the zombie would be in the end with a whip. He would not beat the person. He would instead lash the whip. They made a whip out of rope and would smack the strap on the ground and the zombie would have his head down and keep going until he gets to the area".

The story continues, "Zombie workers would keep about a dozen zombies with them; they would have secret places underground or in a cave somewhere. One room is reserved primarily for the Zombies. They put the zombies in this area and fed them during the day, and during the night, the zombies would go into the fields and work for them. "They do not want them to work during the day, said the storyteller, because they did not want other people to see the zombies. As a result, the crops would produce more and crush the competition.

The story goes, that is how they used the zombies. Sometimes it doesn't work; sometimes, they exhume a body, then find out that it's too late, the body is dead, and they have lost everything. They hardly ever let someone turn back to life because they do not want people to learn what happens, but some stories about people have come back to life. So, they would call the priests in, and the priest would tell them that they would say a prayer for them, but the priests themselves knew what potion to counteract the first medicine. So, they would give that drink to the person who had been a zombie, and that person would return to life. Then the next guy, and that is how they used the zombies.

Robert Brutus

The Zombie stories were not what made our summer vacation memorable. It was the closeness that I had with my grandpa and other relatives. Life was simple. We did not have electricity, nor did we have cell phones, grocery stores, and all the other so-called beautiful amenities we have today. My Grandpa instituted a sense of purity that was very rare to me. I saw a religious man who greatly admired God and his family. I learned to be respectful of others, especially the elderly. In that community, people had a profound appreciation for many things we take for granted today—the value of neighbors and the esteem for authorities.

Chapter 66

Food of Haiti

Though it differs in many ways, Haitian cuisine is like other Caribbean countries in terms of flavor and scent. Like different regional fashions, it is notably unique to the nation and is popular with island tourists.

Despite the modest and straightforward cooking, the tastes are intense and sometimes spicy, demonstrating a fundamental influence from African culinary art where they harmonize with an unmistakable French refinement and crucial byproducts from native Taino and Spanish cooking methods. Season foods liberally and add peppers and herbs to enhance the flavor.

I vaguely recall the amount of work necessary to make a quality supper when I became independent. I never sat down in front of a stove to try to make any meals when I was a kid. Call it good fortune or a blessing, but I had a delightful mother who always ensured food was on the table.

Over the years, I developed a certain level of expertise, at least to my taste, in combining the right amount of rice and beans, cornmeal with black beans, and chicken.

My favorite scent is roasting garlic and onions with quality olive oil. I cannot find any outstanding chefs on the island of Haiti to compile a list of fantastic dishes, so I urge you to check the internet for some beautiful recipes; you will not be disappointed.

In conclusion, many lives come to mind when I ponder the peak events that compose my life's history and also have contributed to the person I am now.

My everyday anxiety enabled me to do incredible things in life. Similarly, the tragedies and upheavals I faced as a young person pushed me to face whatever obstacles life threw. When everything started to fall apart, I returned to my happy place, the music, and the songs I loved the most. If you take the time to count your blessings, you will always have something to grab onto when you are weak.

When dealing with my siblings later in life, the regrettable arguments between my father and his brother were quite helpful. Therefore, learning that my father would go to any length to secure my life while I was unwell as a baby was immensely comforting. I also had an open mind to meet obstacles because of my mother's and father's partly religious upbringing and my father's voodoo background.

You may recall when You had to travel for the first time with your mother or father as a youngster. You always take something away from that experience. When you think about it, you get a wonderful, happy feeling.

Growing up in a world of shared myths, superstitions, and spiritual experiences only served to confuse me on my spiritual path. I found it strange to see my father embrace the significance of a wedding to a mythological person while also trying to rationalize the need to marry my mother.

One of the gutsiest people I know is my father. As often as was required, he defended and shielded us. He was willing to protect us regardless of whether my siblings or I were ill or faced various threats.

I saw my parents go through some steps to treat my sister when she fell ill. It was both an exciting and poignant revelation.

Seeing how close I came to passing away from this world after losing Carlos in the electrocution event let me realize how God had protected me even while I wasn't conscious of his presence.

I carried that information with me at every turn and used it to arrive at many essential decisions after friends exposed me to the Bible and guided me on a path of enlightenment.

I had difficulties before comprehending the political climate, despite my mid-'70s plans to move to the United States.

Later in life, when I tried to compare the political climates in Haiti and the United States, I could identify some parallels, but the two countries are still quite distinct. A dictatorial system sometimes seems to work when everything else fails in Haiti. Whatever regime is in place, Haitians will always be proud of their 1804 declaration of independence.

There will always be groups of individuals in the United States who sincerely feel that things might or ought to be different, which is one of the weaknesses of a democratic system.

Due to the dictatorship of Duvalier's Tonton Macoute, the frequent change of administrations, and the continuing hurricane seasons, Haiti was in a challenging position.

Every time a government has fallen, the people of Haiti have always recovered. Regardless, the event occurs because of an assassination or a hurricane.

The islanders usually recover by setting up a market with the least amount of goods they can find. Even when gaming took control, maintaining life required survival.

When my father left, I adopted his attitude and started acting that way. I didn't let my sorrow over his passing prevent me from doing my job. Instead, I processed the incident slowly and wept afterward.

As you are undoubtedly aware, the 2010 earthquake ravaged the island. The president's murder in 2021 caused more instability. People have continued to suffer, and I do not have any doubt they will recover. So, whatever happens to you, I hope you will recover and pass on your experience to others.

Chapter 67

A Woman to Remember

My mother passed away on April 4th, 2015. I had the chance to say the following about her:

Marie Rose Elizabeth Arius Jean was born On October 31, 1931, in Gressier, Leogane, 12 miles from Port-au-Prince, part of the Léogâne District, Morne-Chandelle sector, Léogâne commune.

She was the firstborn child from a family of four sisters and one brother.

Her parents raised her as an Episcopalian. Her father, an elder of the church, oversaw the regular Sunday mass and Vespers, the sunset evening prayer session, while the official Priest was unavailable. I was so used to seeing my grandfather in priest uniform I grew up believing she was an ordained minister.

She was the bravest woman, wife, mother, and grandma, anybody, could ever have. She has been through a slew of misfortunes in her life. She has always been delighted to tell her kids about the shame she had endured for giving birth to her first son on April Fool's Day, especially because she was not yet married.

The customary plots ranged from folks cracking jokes nonstop to very excruciating teases.

One of the most memorable moments I can remember: I was around six years old, and I observed how heroic to me she was for the first time. There was political unrest between Leogane and Port-au-Prince, and people couldn't travel using any transport vehicle.

After waiting for countless hours for transportation, she decided to start walking. Mind you, she and I, a six-year-old, had already walked for two hours from her father's house to the usual location of procuring transport to Port-au-Prince. The situation had compelled Marie Rose to walk another four hours to ensure I would not miss school the next day.

Marie Rose was an extraordinarily gentle and wonderful mother to be around. She always knew what would please his children and made sure to supply the best of for them.

When a large earthquake devastated Haiti in January 2001, a 7.0 Magnitude Quake occurred near Port au Prince. According to current information, the earthquake affected 3,500,000 people, 220,000 people perished, and 300,000 or more were wounded. The quake damaged over 188,383 dwellings and destroyed 105,000 (293,383 in total), displacing 1.5 million people.

Marie Rose was half-blind and lived in a two-story house at the time. She was upstairs and unable to move when the earthquake struck.

Later, when travel from the United States to Haiti became available, I went to look at the ruins. Eyewitnesses to the tragedy informed me later where they discovered her among the debris. I still couldn't believe how she was able to survive. She survived with minor injuries by the grace of God.

For several weeks, like everyone else, she had to sleep outside since there was no house safe enough as the earthquake's aftershocks continued terrorizing everyone.

Chapter 68

Book Summary

Frantic Souls illustrates how strong and brave people can be while leading happy lives through and after a succession of bizarre, unfortunate, and joyful occurrences in a young child's life through adulthood.

The book explores the conflict between two separate families' allegiances to voodoo and Christianity. The tragic circumstances involving a sick child, the father's union with the spirit world, the challenges of becoming a Christian, the anguish and suffering of a struggling society, and natural calamities are all covered.

Frantic souls revealed the fundamental character of living in a dictatorship society. The author tries to avoid making this narrative become an autobiography while attempting to share actual occurrences. Instead, a collection of stories from various real-life events made the character a sincere follower of Christ. Despite everything, the young child developed into a handy adult in a faraway civilization.

Chapter 69

Acknowledgments

Writing this book has been a once-in-a-lifetime experience for my family and me. This endeavor began when I was still in college. For a long time, I wished to leave a glimpse of my childhood experiences for my children. As memory serves, I scribbled down key events that left an indelible imprint on my psyche.

Because English is not my first language, the assistance I obtained from various individuals made this book more edible, yet it was far from flawless. First and foremost, I want to thank all my children, especially my wife, Phyllis. She has taken the time to go through my phrases and forms regularly.

I'd also like to express my heartfelt gratitude to my daughter Celeste. She took time out of her class schedule to review numerous chapters from the book and gave helpful comments and constructive critiques because she was the closest in terms of location. I'd also want to thank my brother, Spencer, who read the entire book and provided some valuable ideas. Teresa McCallion, a Washington State Department of Health colleague, deserves my heartfelt gratitude. She helped edit a few passages of the book. Finally, I want to convey my sincere appreciation and gratitude to my great friend Randy Rasmusen, who took the time to compose the Preface to this book. Randy's friendship has been beneficial throughout the years.

Chapter 70

Frantic Souls

Resiliency Factor through life adversities

Last updated on: Saturday, Wednesday, January 25, 2023

Frantic Souls

Resiliency in life

Last updated on: Friday, October 7, 2022